This Book belongs to _____

Gift From _____

Date _____

THE SECRET
POWER
OF SPEAKING GOD'S WORD

><

JOYCE MEYER

New York   Boston   Nashville

Unless otherwise noted Scriptures are taken from *The Amplified Bible* (AMP). *The Amplified Bible, Old Testament*, copyright © 1965, 1987 by The Zondervan Corporation. *The Amplified New Testament*, copyright © 1954, 1958, 1987 by The Lockman Foundation. Used by Permission.

Scriptures noted (THE MESSAGE) are taken from *The Message: The Prophets* by Eugene Peterson. Copyright © 2000 by Eugene H. Peterson. NavPress Publishing Group, P.O. Box 35001, Colorado Springs, CO 80935. Used by permission.

Scriptures noted (NIV) are taken from the *Holy Bible: New International Version*®. Copyright © 1973, 1978, 1984 by International Bible Society. Used by permission of Zondervan Publishing House. All rights reserved.

Scripture quotations marked (NKJV) are taken from the *New King James Version*. Copyright © 1979, 1980, 1982 by Thomas Nelson, Inc., Publishers.

Scriptures noted (TLB) are taken from *The Living Bible*, Copyright © 1971. Used by permission of Tyndale House Publishers, Inc., Wheaton, Illinois 60189. All rights reserved.

Scripture quotations marked (NLT) are taken from the *Holy Bible*, New Living Translation, Copyright © 1996. Used by permission of Tyndale House Publishers, Inc., Wheaton, Illinois 60189. All rights reserved.

Scripture quotations marketed (GNT) are taken from the *Good News Translation—Second Edition*, Copyright © 1992, by the American Bible Society. Used by permission. All rights reserved.

Scriptures noted (CEV) are taken from the *Contemporary English Version*, Copyright © 1995 by the American Bible Society. Used by permission.

FaithWords
Hachette Book Group
237 Park Avenue
New York, NY 10017

www.faithwords.com

Printed in the United States of America

Originally published in hardcover by Warner Faith

Deluxe Edition: June 2012
10 9 8 7 6 5 4

FaithWords is a division of Hachette Book Group, Inc.
The FaithWords name and logo are trademarks of Hachette Book Group, Inc.

ISBN: 9781455506200

CONTENTS

INTRODUCTION

✤ Do You Want to Know a Secret? ✤

Everybody does! And I have discovered a powerful secret that I want to share with you—a secret that literally changed my life.

In 1976 God graciously granted me revelation on the power of confessing His Word out loud. Prior to 1976 I was a very negative person who always had negative things to say. Due to abuse in my past and growing up in a very negative atmosphere, my outlook on life was: "If I don't expect anything good to happen to me, then I won't be disappointed when it doesn't."

God had been dealing with me about the very destructive problem of being negative, and I had made a lot of progress in changing the way I thought and spoke. I was careful not to speak negatively, but I was not yet experiencing the positive changes in my life I desired. One day as I was talking to the Lord—basically complaining because I felt I had stopped being negative and had not seen positive changes—I sensed God speaking to my heart: "Joyce, you have stopped saying *negative* things, but you have not started saying *positive* things." It is good to stop doing wrong things, but the real harvest comes in our lives when we plant seed by doing the right thing.

Instantly I knew in my spirit what I needed to do. I spent the next few days compiling a "confession list." It consisted of Scriptures from God's Word and changes that I wanted to see happen in my life. I made sure everything I was planning to confess was in agreement with God's Word. For most of my confessions I actually had chapter and verse to back them up. Using that list, I began confessing God's Word out loud twice a day. I can honestly say that was the beginning of wonderful changes in me, my family, and my life.

Romans 4:17 states that God speaks life to the dead and calls nonexistent things as if they already existed. I began doing the same thing. I was calling those things that did not yet exist in my life into being by confessing God's Word. I must stress that the things I confessed are in God's Word—they were not just things that I had decided I wanted. Confessing God's Word is not a way to get our own will accomplished but, rather, the will of God. As we believe and confess God's Word we are setting ourselves in agreement with Him for His plan to come to pass in our lives.

✦ Open Your Mouth ✦

As one acquaintance of mine says, you cannot defeat Goliath with your mouth shut. We all have enemies or giants in our lives that need to be defeated. First Samuel 17:42-48 tells us that when David was preparing to do battle with the giant Goliath, he ran toward him confessing out loud what he believed the end result of the battle would be.

> *Then said David to the Philistine, You come to me with a sword, a spear, and a javelin, but I come to you in the name of the Lord of hosts, the God of the ranks of Israel, Whom you have defied. This day the Lord will deliver you into my hand, and I will smite you and cut off your head. And I will give the corpses of the army of the Philistines this day to the birds of the air and the wild beasts of the earth, that all the earth may know that there is a God in Israel.*
>
> —1 SAMUEL 17:45-46

We can easily see from David's example how we should approach the enemies that we face in our own lives. We must open our mouth and speak the Word of God.

He prophesied the end result from the beginning of the event. God does the same thing
according to His Word.

> [Earnestly] remember the former things,
> [which I did] of old; for I am God, and there
> is no one else; I am God, and there is none
> like Me, Declaring the end and the result
> from the beginning, and from ancient times
> the things that are not yet done, saying, My
> counsel shall stand, and I will do all My
> pleasure and purpose.
>
> —ISAIAH 46:9-10

You have heard [these things foretold], now you see
this fulfillment. And will you not bear witness to
it? I show you specified new things from this time
forth, even hidden things [kept in reserve] which
you have not known. They are created now [called
into being by the prophetic word]. . . .

—ISAIAH 48:6-7

✸ Ministering Angels ✸

We also have angels available to help us, and
they hearken to the voice of God's Word.

> *Are not the angels all ministering spirits*
> *(servants) sent out in the service [of God for*
> *the assistance] of those who are to inherit*
> *salvation?*
>
> —HEBREWS 1:14

> *Bless (affectionately, gratefully praise) the*
> *Lord, you His angels, you mighty ones who*
> *do His commandments, hearkening to the*
> *voice of His word.*
>
> —PSALM 103:20

This is exciting! When we confess God's
Word out loud, the angels hear it and go to
work for us. It is easy to see we cannot defeat
the enemy unless we wield the two-edged
sword of God's Word. As David ran *toward*

Goliath (not away from him), the Word was going forth out of his mouth, and angels were activated to assist him.

The angels are not activated by our complaining, murmuring, doubting, and unbelief. They want to work on our behalf, that is their assignment from God, but we need to release them by speaking or praying God's Word.

⍟ A Spiritual Discipline ⍟

Just as we need natural disciplines such as discipline to work and disciplines concerning appetites, finances, and so on, we also need spiritual disciplines such as prayer, Bible study, and confessing God's Word out loud. We may not always want to, but as we discipline ourselves to do these things, they will become habits. Then we will see good results just as we see good results from any other discipline that is applied over a period of time. Doing something good one time does not produce long-lasting good results. Discipline doesn't produce immediate joy, but it is an investment that will pay great dividends in due time. (Hebrews 12:11).

I strongly encourage you to confess the Word of God out loud daily—even two or three times a day, or throughout the day as the Holy Spirit prompts you. Each time a thought comes to your mind that does not agree with God's Word, confess the truth of God's Word out loud, and you will find the wrong thought disappearing.

Second Corinthians 10:4-5 teaches us that our weapons are not carnal, but are mighty through God to the pulling down of strongholds in our mind. Casting down imaginations, thoughts, reasonings, and theories that don't agree with God's Word requires us to use our offensive weapon—the Word of God coming out of our mouth. When we speak, it becomes a two-edged sword that defeats the enemy with one edge and opens the blessings of heaven with the other. There are many other weapons that are *defensive*, but the Word is *offensive*—it chases the enemy, driving him back.

Like any other principle in God's Word, this will not work if it is not applied. Just knowing it doesn't change anything. Faith is active. It must be released. We can release God's Word through prayer, confessing His Word out loud, and taking God-inspired action. We are blessed in the "doing" not just the "knowing." James 2:17 says, "faith without works is dead."

Do not look at confessing God's Word out loud as a formula for getting everything you want. Do it in faith, knowing it pleases God when we agree with His word. Enter God's rest concerning the timing of the results. God is faithful and as we continue to do our part. He never fails to do His. When I began confessing the Word out loud in 1976, changes in my life did not come overnight. But gradually I did see changes, and still to this day I always see good results from verbalizing my faith and speaking in agreement with God.

In Psalm 45:1 David said that his tongue was as the pen of a ready writer. And in Proverbs 3:1, 3 the Word states that we should not forget God's laws but write them on the tablet of our heart. We see from these two Scriptures that our heart is the tablet and our tongue is the pen. When we confess God's Word out loud, we write it on our own heart, and it becomes more firmly established both in our heart and in the earth. God's Word is forever settled in heaven (see Psalm 119:89), and we establish it in the earth each time we speak it.

I know that my husband, Dave, loves me, but each time I hear him say, "I love you," it is more firmly established in my life. So it is with this spiritual principle.

✦ The Pattern ✦

We see a pattern for this principle in the book of Romans, which teaches us that in order to be saved, we must believe in our heart and confess with our mouth.

> *Because if you acknowledge and confess with your lips that Jesus is Lord and in your heart believe (adhere to, trust in, and rely on the truth) that God raised Him from the dead, you will be saved. For with the heart a person believes (adheres to, trusts in, and relies on Christ) and so is justified (declared righteous, acceptable to God) and with the mouth he confesses (declares openly and speaks out freely his faith) and confirms [his] salvation.*
>
> —ROMANS 10:9-10

So I say we should believe and speak, speak and believe—the two work together!

❧ Hold Fast Your Confession ❧

Hebrews 4:14 and 10:23 both tell us to hold fast our confession of faith in Him. When we hold fast to something, it indicates that something or someone is trying to take it away from us. Satan will try to steal our confession by putting wrong thoughts in our mind, hoping the thoughts will produce wrong words that will come out of our mouth. The power of life and death is in the tongue, and we eat the fruit of our words, whether for life or death (see Proverbs 18:21).

Satan will tell us that confessing the Word does no good, that it changes nothing. He will cause us to forget to do it or to feel lazy and just not want to do it even though we know we should. He will cause us to get weary of doing it. Satan fights anything that will produce good results in our lives.

To confess means "to say the same thing as . . . to agree with or assent to." We need to say the same thing as God says and get into agreement with Him so that His good plan for our lives can come to pass.

First Timothy 6:12 instructs us to fight the good fight of faith. We must fight battles and press in to do what God tells us to do.

⚜ God's Word Does Not Return Void ⚜

Isaiah teaches us that the Word coming out of God's mouth (which I believe can also be our mouths dedicated to Him) will not return void. It accomplishes what it was sent to do. The Word of God is seed, and when we release it in the earth, we will see good results.

For as the rain and snow come down from the heavens, and return not there again, but water the earth and make it bring forth and sprout, that it may give seed to the sower and bread to the eater, So shall My word be that goes forth out of My mouth: it shall not return to Me void [without producing any effect, useless] but it shall accomplish that which I please and purpose, and it shall prosper in the thing for which I sent it.

—ISAIAH 55:10-11

We are God's representatives in the earth, His mouthpieces, and we are instructed by the apostle Paul to imitate Him. As His representatives, we should speak His Word just the same as He would. We should speak it boldly, with authority, believing it has power to change our lives and circumstances.

This principle has been life-changing for me. There were times when I let the principle slip away, but the Holy Spirit was always faithful to remind me to confess His Word. There are seasons when I spend more time than usual confessing God's Word out loud. Yet I can say with certainty it has been a regular part of my daily life throughout all these years. I don't believe I would be where I am today had I not applied this powerful biblical principle in my life.

This book contains powerful Scriptures arranged in an alphabetical topical format that allows you to quickly and easily begin confessing the Word out loud regarding your specific need(s). Make it a spiritual discipline. Release your faith as you release the Scriptures out of your mouth, and get ready to see wonderful changes in your life.

And He said to me, Son of man, can these bones live? And I answered, O Lord God, You know! Again He said to me, Prophesy to these bones and say to them, O you dry bones, hear the word of the Lord. . . . So I prophesied as I was commanded; and as I prophesied, there was a [thundering] noise and behold, a shaking and trembling and a rattling, and the bones came together, bone to its bone. . . . So I prophesied as He commanded me, and the breath and spirit

*came into [the bones], and they lived and
stood up upon their feet, an exceedingly
great host.*

—EZEKIEL 37:3-4, 7, 10

These Scriptures are a striking example of how
things can change by prophesying (speaking
forth) God's Word.

*God's Word spoken out of your mouth
regularly produces a powerful, victorious life!*

Now you know the secret—the power of
the Word is unleashed when you speak it
out—so make a decision and get started
today!

⭒ How To Use This Book ⭒

You will notice that I have worded most of
the confessions in first person for your ease in
making them personal to you and your life.

They are either taken directly from a Scripture or have a Scriptural basis in God's word.

The Scriptures are listed in categories I feel people will need the most at various times in their lives. I suggest that you use them frequently. Confessing the Word regularly is like a sick person taking their medicine regularly.

> *My son, attend to my words; consent and submit to my sayings. Let them not depart from your sight; keep them in the center of your heart. For they are life to those who find them, healing and health to all their flesh.*
> —PROVERBS 4:20-22

These Scriptures imply that God's Word works in us as medicine does in the flesh or body of a sick individual.

You can confess the Word in any area simply to keep it alive in your heart. Confess it for maintenance or to keep you strong in specific areas. You can and should also choose sections to confess and meditate on in which you are having problems. If you are repeatedly experiencing impatience, you can open the book to the section on patience and make it a matter of study, confession, and meditation. Likewise, if you are struggling with forgiveness, spend time confessing the Scriptures in the section on forgiving others.

The Word is like medicine but it is most effective when applied properly. If I have a headache, I don't put a Band-Aid on my head. If I cut myself, I don't put an aspirin in the cut. We know how to apply medicine in the natural and should learn to do so spiritually. If I wake up feeling extremely short tempered and grouchy, it won't help me to listen to a teaching tape or read a book on prosperity and success. I need something about walking in love and the fruit of the Spirit.

If you apply the Word to your life just as you would medicine to a wound or sickness you will be amazed at the power which will be unleashed in your life.

I believe I have provided you with a wonderful Word dictionary to help you begin your new life of meditating on and confessing God's Word out loud on a regular basis. These confessions are meant to provide a foundation for you, but you should add those that are pertinent to your own life and situations.

I want to reiterate how important this principle and spiritual discipline has been in my own life. I sincerely pray you will not just read this book and put it on a shelf. I encourage you to use it daily. I believe you will be strengthened in faith and have the joy of witnessing many manifestations of God's goodness and power.

In Psalm 138:2 we see God has exalted above all else His Word and His Name, and He has magnified His Word even above His Name. That says a lot! The Word of God is a treasure. As we hear it, learn it, receive it, believe it, and speak it, we are making an investment that will pay glorious dividends in our lives. May God richly bless you as you make progress in exalting His Word above all else.

Speaking God's Word about . . .

⁂ Anger ⁂

I will bridle my anger, trash my wrath, cool my pipes—it only makes things worse.

—PSALM 37:8 (THE MESSAGE)

I follow the example of the Lord, who is merciful and gracious, slow to anger and plenteous in mercy and loving-kindness.

—PSALM 103:8

I am slow to anger and have great understanding; I am not like he who is hasty of spirit, exposing and exalting his folly.

—PROVERBS 14:29

I speak soft answers that turn away wrath, not grievous words that stir up anger.

—PROVERBS 15:1

I am not a hot-tempered person who stirs up strife, but I am slow to anger, appeasing contention.

—PROVERBS 15:18

Good sense makes me restrain my anger, and it is my glory to overlook a transgression or an offense.

—PROVERBS 19:11

I am not quick in spirit to be angry or vexed, for anger and vexation lodge in the bosom of fools.

—ECCLESIASTES 7:9

When I am angry, I do not sin or let my wrath (my exasperation, my fury or indignation) last until the sun goes down.

—EPHESIANS 4:26

I will let all bitterness and indignation and wrath (passion, rage, bad temper) and resentment (anger, animosity) and quarreling (brawling, clamor, contention) and slander (evil-speaking, abusive or blasphemous language) be banished from me, with all malice (spite, ill will, or baseness of any kind). And I will become useful and helpful and kind to others, tenderhearted (compassionate, understanding, loving-hearted), forgiving others [readily and freely], as God in Christ forgave me.

—EPHESIANS 4:31-32

Now I must get rid of all these things: anger, passion, and hateful feelings. No insults or obscene talk must ever come from my lips.

—COLOSSIANS 3:8 (GNT)

I won't forget that it is best to listen much, speak little, and not become angry; for anger doesn't make me good, as God demands that I must be.

—JAMES 1:19-20 (TLB)

⚜ Anointing ⚜

Now I know that the Lord saves His
anointed; He will answer me from His holy
heaven with the saving strength of His right
hand.

—PSALM 20:6

You anoint my head with oil; my [brimming]
cup runs over.

—PSALM 23:5

I love righteousness, uprightness, and right
standing with God and hate wickedness;
therefore God, My God, has anointed me
with the oil of gladness.

—PSALM 45:7

My horn (emblem of excessive strength and
stately grace) You have exalted; I am anointed
with fresh oil.

—PSALM 92:10

And it shall come to pass in that day, that his burden shall be taken away from off thy shoulder, and his yoke from off thy neck, and the yoke shall be destroyed because of the anointing.

—ISAIAH 10:27 (KJV)

The Spirit of the Lord God is upon me, because the Lord has anointed me to bring good news to the suffering and afflicted. He has sent me to comfort the brokenhearted, to announce liberty to captives, and to open the eyes of the blind.

—ISAIAH 61:1 (TLB)

Like Jesus' disciples, I am called to drive out many unclean spirits and anoint with oil many who are sick and cure them.

—MARK 6:13

It is God Who confirms and makes me steadfast and establishes me in Christ, and has

consecrated and anointed me [enduing me
with the gifts of the Holy Spirit].

—2 CORINTHIANS 1:21

I have been anointed by the Holy one, and I
know [the Truth].

—1 JOHN 2:20

But as for me, the anointing (the sacred
appointment, the unction) which I received
from Him abides [permanently] in me; [so]
then I have no need that anyone should
instruct me. But just as His anointing teaches
me concerning everything and is true and is
no falsehood, so I must abide in (live in, never
depart from) Him [being rooted in Him, knit
to Him], just as [His anointing] has taught me
[to do].

—1 JOHN 2:27

✤ Anxiety and Worry ✤

I am strong, courageous, and firm; I fear not
and am not in terror, for it is the Lord my God
Who goes with me; He will not fail me or
forsake me.

—DEUTERONOMY 31:6

In the day of my trouble I will call to you, for
you will answer me.

—PSALM 86:7 (NIV)

Search me, O God, and know my heart; try
me, and know my anxieties; and see if there
is any wicked way in me, and lead me in the
way everlasting.

—PSALM 139:23-24 (NKJV)

All the days of the desponding and afflicted
are made evil [by anxious thoughts and
forebodings], but I have a glad heart and a
continual feast [regardless of circumstances].

—PROVERBS 15:15

My worrying and being anxious will not add
one unit of measure (cubit) to my stature or
to the span of my life.

—MATTHEW 6:27

I will not worry and be anxious, saying, What
am I going to eat? or, What am I going to
drink? or, What am I going to wear? . . . But I
will seek (aim at and strive after) first of all
His kingdom and His righteousness (His way
of doing and being right), and then all these
things taken together will be given me
besides.

—MATTHEW 6:31, 33

I will not worry or be anxious about
tomorrow, for tomorrow will have worries
and anxieties of its own. Sufficient for each
day is its own trouble.

—MATTHEW 6:34

I will not let the worries of this life, the deceitfulness of wealth and the desires for other things come in and choke the word, making it unfruitful.

—MARK 4:19 (NIV)

I am not anxious about anything, but in everything, by prayer and petition, with thanksgiving, I present my requests to God. And the peace of God, which transcends all understanding, guards my heart and my mind in Christ Jesus.

—PHILIPPIANS 4:6-7 (NIV)

I cast the whole of my care [all my anxieties, all my worries, all my concerns, once and for all] on Him, for He cares for me affectionately and cares about me watchfully.

—1 PETER 5:7

✢ Authority of the Believer ✢

I bind the strongman and I am able to rob his kingdom.

—MATTHEW 12:29

As a disciple of Christ I have the keys of the kingdom of heaven; and whatever I bind on earth is bound and whatever I loose is loosed.

—MATTHEW 16:19

Jesus has all authority and power in heaven and in earth and whatever is His is also mine. He gives me authority to go and make disciples of all nations, baptizing them in the name of the Father, Son and Holy Spirit.

—MATTHEW 28:18-19

I am a believer and these signs follow me: In Jesus' name I drive out demons; speak in new languages; pick up serpents (deal with

demonic powers); and [even] if I drink anything deadly, it will not hurt me; I lay my
hands on the sick, and they recover.

—MARK 16:17-18

God has given me authority and power to
trample upon serpents and scorpions, and
[physical and mental strength and ability]
over all the power that the enemy [pos-
sesses]; and nothing shall in any way harm
me.

—LUKE 10:19

Christ is seated in heavenly places and I am
seated in Him. He is above all principalities
and powers and all things are under His feet.

—EPHESIANS 1:20-22, 2:6 (NKJV)

I submit myself to God, I resist the devil and
He must flee.

—JAMES 4:7 (NKJV)

⸙ Compromise ⸙

I am very, very careful never to compromise
with the people around me and I do not
follow their evil ways.

—EXODUS 34:12 (TLB)

I am blessed, happy, fortunate, prosperous,
and to be envied because I walk and live not
in the counsel of the ungodly [following their
advice, their plans and purposes], nor do I
stand [submissive and inactive] in the path
where sinners walk, nor sit down [to relax
and rest] where the scornful [and the
mockers] gather.

—PSALM 1:1

I search for God and always do His will,
rejecting compromise with evil and walking
only in His paths.

—PSALM 119:2-3 (TLB)

I am a righteous person who does not yield,
fall down or compromise my integrity before
the wicked.

—PROVERBS 25:26

I live before God, doing my duty with a
perfectly good conscience.

—ACTS 23:1

I possess the mystic secret of the faith
[Christian truth as hidden from ungodly men]
with a clear conscience.

—1 TIMOTHY 3:9

I prefer to suffer the hardships of the people
of God rather than to have the fleeting
enjoyment of a sinful life.

—HEBREWS 11:25

I am a member of a chosen race, a royal
priesthood, a dedicated nation, [God's] own

purchased, special person, that I may set forth
the wonderful deeds and display the virtues
and perfections of Him Who called me out of
darkness into His marvelous light.

—1 PETER 2:9

⚜ Civic Responsibility ⚜

For what great nation is there who has a god
so near to them as the Lord our God is to us
in all things for which we call upon Him?
—DEUTERONOMY 4:7

I am one of God's chosen people. I am called
by His name. If I humble myself, pray, seek,
crave, and require of necessity the face of
God and turn from my wicked ways, then
will God hear from heaven, forgive my sin,
and heal my land.
—2 CHRONICLES 7:14

I pray for the peace of Jerusalem! May they
prosper who love you [the Holy City]! May
peace be within your walls and prosperity
within your palaces!
—PSALM 122:6-7

By the blessing of the influence of the upright and God's favor [because of them] the city is exalted, but it is overthrown by the mouth of the wicked.

—PROVERBS 11:11

I [reverently] fear the Lord and the king, and do not associate with those who are given to change [of allegiance, and are revolutionary].

—PROVERBS 24:21

I keep the law [of God and man], and I am wise.

—PROVERBS 28:7

I seek peace and prosperity for my city. I pray to the Lord for it, because the Lord Almighty says that if it prospers, I too prosper.

—JEREMIAH 29:7 (NIV)

I pay to my government the things that are
due to my government, and I pay to God the
things that are due to God.

—MATTHEW 22:21

I am loyally subject to the governing (civil)
authorities. For there is no authority except
from God [by His permission, His sanction],
and those that exist do so by God's appointment.

—ROMANS 13:1

I give everyone what I owe him: If I owe
taxes, I pay taxes; if revenue, then revenue;
if respect, then respect; if honor, then honor.

—ROMANS 13:7 (NIV)

I offer petitions, prayers, intercessions, and
thanksgivings on behalf of all men, for kings
and all who are in positions of authority or
high responsibility, that [outwardly] I may

pass a quiet and undisturbed life [and inwardly] a peaceable one in all godliness and reverence and seriousness in every way. For such [praying] is good and right, and [it is] pleasing and acceptable to God my Savior.

—1 TIMOTHY 2:1-3

I am subject to rulers and authorities, obedient, ready to do whatever is good. I slander no one, I am peaceable and considerate, and I show true humility toward all men.

—TITUS 3:1-2 (NIV)

I make the Master proud of me by being a good citizen. I respect the authorities, whatever their level; they are God's emissaries for keeping order. It is God's will that by doing good, I might cure the ignorance of the fools who think I'm a danger to society. I exercise my freedom by serving God, not by breaking

the rules. I treat everyone I meet with dignity.
I love my spiritual family, revere God, and
respect the government.

—1 PETER 2:13-17 (THE MESSAGE)

⸙ Confessions ⸙

Confessions for Husbands

As for me and my house, we will serve the Lord.

—JOSHUA 24:15 (KJV)

Love and faithfulness never leave me; I bind them around my neck. I write them on the tablet of my heart.

—PROVERBS 3:3 (NIV)

I will live joyfully with the wife whom I love all the days of my life which He has given me under the sun.

—ECCLESIASTES 9:9

From the beginning of creation God made male and female. For this reason I have left [behind] my father and my mother and am joined to my wife and cleave closely to her permanently, and we two have become one flesh, so that we are no longer two, but one flesh. What therefore God has united (joined together), no man will separate or divide.

—MARK 10:6-9

I am not mean, bad-tempered and angry. I will not quarrel and say harsh words. These things should have no place in my life. I am kind to my wife, tenderhearted, forgiving, just as God has forgiven me because I belong to Christ.

—EPHESIANS 4:31-32

I show the same kind of love to my wife as Christ showed to the church when He died for her, to make her holy and clean, washed by baptism and God's Word; so that He could give her to Himself as a glorious church without a single spot or wrinkle or any other blemish, being holy and without a single

fault. That is how husbands should treat their
wives, loving them as parts of themselves.
For since a man and his wife are now one, a
man is really doing himself a favor and loving
himself when he loves his wife!

—EPHESIANS 5:25-28 (TLB)

I put away and rid myself [completely] of all
these things: anger, rage, bad feeling toward
my wife, curses and slander, and foul-
mouthed abuse and shameful utterances from
my lips! I do not lie, for I have stripped off the
old (unregenerate) self with its evil practices,
and have clothed myself as God's own
chosen one. . . . (His own picked representa-
tive), [who is] purified and holy and well-
beloved [by God Himself, by putting on
behavior marked by] tenderhearted pity and
mercy, kind feeling, a lowly opinion of
myself, gentle ways, [and] patience [which is
tireless and long-suffering, and has the power

to endure whatever comes, with good temper]. I am gentle and forbearing, readily pardoning others; even as the Lord has [freely] forgiven me. And above all these [I put on] love and enfold myself and my wife with the bond of perfectness [which binds everything together completely in ideal harmony].

—COLOSSIANS 3:8-10, 12-14

I give honor to [my] marriage, and remain faithful to my wife in marriage.

—HEBREWS 13:4 (NLT)

I confess my faults to my wife, and we pray for one another, that we may be healed. The effectual fervent prayer of a righteous man availeth much.

—JAMES 5:16 (KJV)

I give honor to my wife. I treat her with understanding as we live together. She may be weaker than I am, but she is my equal partner in God's gift of new life. If I don't treat her as I should, my prayers will not be heard.

—1 PETER 3:7 (NLT)

Confessions for Wives

An excellent wife is the crown of her husband. I am an excellent wife.

—PROVERBS 12:4 (NKJV)

House and riches are the inheritance of fathers and a prudent wife is from the Lord. I am a prudent wife.

—PROVERBS 19:14 (KJV)

I am a wife of noble character. I am worth far more than rubies. My husband has full confidence in me and lacks nothing of value. I bring him good, not harm, all the days of my life.

—PROVERBS 31:10-12 (NIV)

I open my mouth with skillful and godly Wisdom, and on my tongue is the law of kindness [giving counsel and instruction].

—PROVERBS 31:26

I am bought with a price: therefore I glorify God in my body, and in my spirit, which are God's.

—1 CORINTHIANS 6:20 (KJV)

The man should give his wife all that is her right as a married woman, and the wife should do the same for her husband.

—1 CORINTHIANS 7:3 (TLB)

I operate in the spiritual gifts toward my husband. Love is patient; I am patient. Love is kind; I am kind. Love does not envy; I do not envy. Love does not boast, it is not proud. I do not boast, I am not proud. Love is not rude, self-seeking, or easily angered, it keeps no record of wrongs. I am not rude, self-seeking, or easily angered. I keep no record of wrongs. Love does not delight in evil but rejoices in the truth. I do not delight in evil but rejoice with the truth. Love always protects, always trusts, always hopes, always perseveres. Love never fails. I always protect, always trust, always hope, always persevere.

—1 CORINTHIANS 13:1-8 (NIV)

I respect and reverence my husband, I notice him, regard him, honor him, prefer him, venerate him, and esteem him. I defer to him, praise him, love and admire him exceedingly.

—EPHESIANS 5:33

I encourage my husband and build him up. I do not pay back wrong for wrong, but always try to be kind to him. I am joyful always. I pray continually; giving thanks in all circumstances, for this is God's will for me in Christ Jesus.

—1 THESSALONIANS 5:11, 15-18 (NIV)

I am worthy of respect and serious, not a gossiper, but temperate and self-controlled, [thoroughly] trustworthy in all things.

—1 TIMOTHY 3:11

I will wisely train the young women to be sane and sober of mind (temperate, disciplined) and to love their husbands and their children, to be self-controlled, chaste, homemakers, good-natured (kindhearted), adapting and subordinating themselves to their husbands, that the word of God may not be exposed to reproach (blasphemed or discredited).

—TITUS 2:4-5

I am submissive to my husband so that he may be won over without words, but by my behavior, when he sees the purity and reverence of my life. I have the unfading beauty of a gentle and quiet spirit, which is of great worth in God's sight. This is the way the holy women of the past who put their hope in God used to make themselves beautiful.

—1 PETER 3:1-5 (NIV)

I love not [merely] in theory or in speech
but in deed and in truth (in practice and in
sincerity).

—1 JOHN 3:18

Confessions for Parents

My children [reverently] fear the Lord, and keep all His statutes and His commandments. . . . They love the Lord their God with all their [mind and] heart and with their entire being and with all their might.

—DEUTERONOMY 6:2, 5

My children are the head, and not the tail; and they shall be above only, and they shall not be beneath, because they heed the commandments of the Lord their God and are watchful to do them.

—DEUTERONOMY 28:13

My children choose life and blessing. They love the Lord, obey His voice, and cling to Him. For He is their life and the length of their days.

—DEUTERONOMY 30:19-20

My children make right choices according to
the Word of God.

—ISAIAH 54:13

Children's children are the crown of old men,
and the glory of children is their fathers.

—PROVERBS 17:6

My children rise up and call me blessed
(happy, fortunate, and to be envied).

—PROVERBS 31:28

As the clay is in the potter's hand, so are my
children in the hands of the Lord.

—JEREMIAH 18:6

I am always a positive encourager. I edify and
build up; I never tear down or destroy.

—ROMANS 15:2

All my children have Christian friends, and God has set aside a Christian wife or husband for each of them.

—1 CORINTHIANS 15:33

My children are not unequally yoked with unbelievers.

—2 CORINTHIANS 6:14

My children walk and live [habitually] in the [Holy] Spirit [responsive to and controlled and guided by the Spirit].

—GALATIANS 5:16

My children have the spirit of wisdom and revelation [of insight into mysteries and secrets] in the [deep and intimate] knowledge of God. Their eyes have been flooded with light, so that they can know and understand the hope to which He has called them, and

how rich is His glorious inheritance in the
saints (His set-apart ones).

—EPHESIANS 1:17-18

My children obey me in the Lord, for this is
right. They honor their father and mother—
which is the first commandment with a
promise—"that it may go well with them and
that they may enjoy long life on the earth."

—EPHESIANS 6:1-3 (NIV)

I do not exasperate my children; instead, I
bring them up in the training and instruction
of the Lord.

—EPHESIANS 6:4 (NIV)

My children do all things without grumbling
and faultfinding and complaining [against
God] and questioning and doubting.

—PHILIPPIANS 2:14

I always thank God, the Father of our Lord
Jesus Christ, when I pray for my children.
They have the faith and love that spring from
the hope that is stored up for them in heaven.
God has filled them with the knowledge of
His will through all spiritual wisdom and
understanding. They live lives worthy of the
Lord and please Him in every way: bearing
fruit in every good work, growing in the
knowledge of God, strengthened with all
power according to His glorious might so that
they may have great endurance and patience,
and joyfully give thanks to the Father. They
are qualified to share in the inheritance of the
saints in the kingdom of light. He has rescued
them from the dominion of darkness and
brought them into the kingdom of the Son He
loves, in whom they have redemption, the
forgiveness of sins.

—COLOSSIANS 1:3, 5, 9-14 (NIV)

My children love to pray and study the Word.
They correctly analyze the Word of Truth.

—2 TIMOTHY 2:15

My children have a teachable spirit.

—PROVERBS 14:16 (AMP)

Confessions for Singles

The Lord is a shield for me, my glory, and the lifter of my head. With my voice I cry to the Lord, and He hears and answers me out of His holy hill. Selah [I pause, and calmly think of that]!

—PSALM 3:3-4

One thing have I asked of the Lord, that will I seek, inquire for, and [insistently] require: that I may dwell in the house of the Lord [in His presence] all the days of my life, to behold and gaze upon the beauty [the sweet attractiveness and the delightful loveliness] of the Lord and to meditate, consider, and inquire in His temple.

—PSALM 27: 4

I wait and hope for and expect the Lord; I am brave and of good courage and let my heart

be stout and enduring. Yes, I wait for and
hope for and expect the Lord.

—PSALM 27:14

I fret not myself, neither am I envious.

—PSALM 37:1

I trust (lean on, rely on, and am confident) in
the Lord and do good; so shall I dwell in the
land and feed surely on His faithfulness, and
truly I shall be fed. I delight myself in the
Lord, and He gives me the desires and secret
petitions of my heart. I commit my way to
the Lord [roll and repose each care of my load
on Him]; trust (lean on, rely on, and am confident) also in Him and He will bring it to pass.

—PSALM 37:3-5

I give my burdens to the Lord, and He will
take care of me. He will not permit me to slip
and fall.

—PSALM 55:22 (NLT)

Because I have set my love upon God,
therefore will He deliver me; He will set me
on high, because I know and understand His
name [have a personal knowledge of His
mercy, love, and kindness—trust and rely on
Him, knowing He will never forsake me, no,
never]. I shall call upon God, and He will
answer me; He will be with me in trouble, He
will deliver me and honor me. With long life
will the Lord satisfy me and show me His
salvation.

—PSALM 91:14-16

The end of a thing is better than its beginning, and the patient in spirit is better than
the proud in spirit. I do not hasten in my
spirit to be angry, for anger rests in the bosom
of fools.

—ECCLESIASTES 7:8-9 (NKJV)

I fear not, for the Lord has redeemed me; He
has called me by my name. I am His. When I

pass through the waters, He will be with me; and through the rivers, they shall not overflow me. When I walk through the fire, I shall not be burned, nor shall the flame scorch me. For the Holy One of Israel is my Savior.

—ISAIAH 43:1-3 (NKJV)

The Spirit of the Lord God is upon me, because the Lord has anointed and qualified me to preach the Gospel of good tidings to the meek, the poor, and afflicted; He has sent me to bind up and heal the brokenhearted, to proclaim liberty to the [physical and spiritual] captives and the opening of the prison and of the eyes to those who are bound. To proclaim the acceptable year of the Lord [the year of His favor] and the day of vengeance of our God, to comfort all who mourn, to grant [consolation and joy] to those who mourn in Zion—to give them an ornament (a garland or diadem) of beauty instead of ashes, the oil of joy instead of mourning, the garment [expressive] of praise instead of a heavy, burdened, and failing spirit....

—ISAIAH 61:1-3

Then will the maidens rejoice in the dance, and the young men and old together. For God will turn my mourning into joy and will comfort me and make me rejoice after my sorrow.

—JEREMIAH 31:13

Jesus said He would be with me always, even to the end of the age. I am not alone. Jesus promised to be with me always.

—MATTHEW 28:20 (NKJV)

But if we hope for that we see not, then do we with patience wait for it.

—ROMANS 8:25 (KJV)

I cast the whole of my care [all my anxieties, all my worries, all my concerns, once and for all] on Him, for He cares for me affectionately and cares about me watchfully.

—1 PETER 5:7

Confessions for Families

As for me and my house, we will serve the
Lord.

—JOSHUA 24:15

Through skillful and godly Wisdom is my
house (life, home, family) built, and by
understanding it is established [on a sound
and good foundation], and by knowledge
shall its chambers [of every area] be filled
with all precious and pleasant riches.

—PROVERBS 24:3-4

I commit my family to God [I deposit them in
His charge, entrusting them to His protection
and care]. And I commend them to the Word
of His grace [to the commands and counsels
and promises of His unmerited favor]. It is
able to build my family up and to give us [our
rightful] inheritance among all God's set-apart

ones (those consecrated, purified, and transformed of soul).

—ACTS 20:32

I bless God, the Father of our Lord Jesus Christ (the Messiah) Who has blessed my family in Christ with every spiritual (given by the Holy Spirit) blessing in the heavenly realm!

—EPHESIANS 1:3

My family is gentle and forbearing with one another and, if one has a difference (a grievance or complaint) against another, we readily pardon each other; even as the Lord has [freely] forgiven us, so must we also [forgive]. And above all these we [put on] love and enfold ourselves with the bond of perfectness [which binds everything together completely in ideal harmony]. And we let the peace (soul harmony which comes) from

Christ rule (act as umpire continually) in our hearts [deciding and settling with finality all questions that arise in our minds, in that peaceful state] to which as [members of Christ's] one body we were also called [to live]. And we are thankful (appreciative), [giving praise to God always].

—COLOSSIANS 3:13-15

My family loves one another, for love is (springs) from God; and he who loves [his family] is begotten (born) of God and is coming [progressively] to know and under- stand God [to perceive and recognize and get a better and clearer knowledge of Him]. My family loves God so [very much], we also ought to love one another, and we do.

—1 JOHN 4:7, 11

My family is healthy and prosperous. Everything we lay our hand to is blessed.

—3 JOHN 2 & DEUTERONOMY 28:8, 11-12

What the Bible Says about
Confessing the Word

This Book of the Law shall not depart out of my mouth, but I shall meditate on it day and night, that I may observe and do according to all that is written in it. For then the Lord shall make my way prosperous, and then I shall deal wisely and have good success.

—JOSHUA 1:8

Thy word is a lamp unto my feet, and a light unto my path.

—PSALM 119:105 (KJV)

God shows me specified new things from this time forth, even hidden things [kept in reserve] which I have not known. They are created now [called into being by the prophetic word].

—ISAIAH 48:6-7

The Word of God that I speak from my mouth will not return to Him empty, but will accomplish what He desires and achieve the purpose for which He sent it to me.

—ISAIAH 55:11 (NIV)

The Lord watches over His word to perform it.

—JEREMIAH 1:12

As it is written, I have made you the father of many nations. [He was appointed our father] in the sight of God in Whom he believed, Who gives life to the dead and speaks of the non-existent things that [He has foretold and promised] as if they [already] existed.

—ROMANS 4:17

The Word that God speaks is alive and full of power [making it active, operative, energizing, and effective]; it is sharper than any two-edged sword, penetrating to the dividing line of the breath of life (soul) and [the immortal] spirit, and of joints and marrow [of the deepest parts of our nature], exposing and sifting and analyzing and judging the very thoughts and purposes of the heart.

—HEBREWS 4:12

So [it shall be] that he who invokes a blessing on himself in the land shall do so by saying, May the God of truth and fidelity [the Amen] bless me; and he who takes an oath in the land shall swear by the God of truth and faithfulness to His promises [the Amen], because the former troubles are forgotten and because they are hidden from My eyes.

—ISAIAH 65:16

When I say to this mountain, Be lifted up and thrown into the sea! and I do not doubt at all in my heart but believe that what I say will take place, it will be done for me.

—MARK 11:23

Inasmuch then as we have a great High Priest
Who has [already] ascended and passed
through the heavens, Jesus the Son of God, I
hold fast my confession [of faith in Him].

—HEBREWS 4:14

I seize and hold fast and retain without
wavering the hope I cherish and confess and
my acknowledgement of it, for He Who
promised is reliable (sure) and faithful to His
word.

—HEBREWS 10:23

⸎ Confidence ⸎

I am determined and confident! I am not
afraid or discouraged, for the Lord my God is
with me wherever I go.

—JOSHUA 1:9 (GNT)

With your help I can advance against a troop;
with my God I can scale a wall.

—PSALM 18:29 (NIV)

I trust (lean on, rely on, and am confident) in
the Lord and do good; so shall I dwell in the
land and feed surely on His faithfulness, and
truly I shall be fed.

—PSALM 37:3

My heart is fixed, O God, my heart is
steadfast and confident! I will sing and make
melody.

—PSALM 57:7

O Lord of hosts, I am blessed (happy, fortunate, to be envied) because I trust in You [leaning and believing on You, committing all and confidently looking to You, and that without fear or misgiving]!

—PSALM 84:12

I don't concern myself with matters too great or awesome for me. But I have stilled and quieted myself, just as a small child is quiet with its mother.

—PSALM 131:1-2 (NLT)

The fear of man brings a snare, but I lean on, trust in, and put my confidence in the Lord and I'm safe and set on high.

—PROVERBS 29:25

God guards me, keeps me in perfect and constant peace because my mind [both its inclination and its character] is stayed on

Him, because I commit myself to Him, lean on Him, and hope confidently in Him.

—ISAIAH 26:3

In quietness and in trusting confidence I find strength.

—ISAIAH 30:15

I will look to the Lord and confident in Him I will keep watch; I will wait with hope and expectancy for the God of my salvation; my God will hear me.

—MICAH 7:7

I am confident of this very thing, that He who has begun a good work in me will complete it until the day of Jesus Christ.

—PHILIPPIANS 1:6 (NKJV)

I put no confidence in the flesh or on outward privileges and physical advantages and

external appearances. I put my confidence in
Jesus Christ and I glory in Him.

—PHILIPPIANS 3:3

I approach the throne of grace with confidence, so that I may receive mercy and find
grace to help me in my time of need.

—HEBREWS 4:16 (NIV)

I do not fling away my fearless confidence,
for it carries a great and glorious compensa-
tion of reward.

—HEBREWS 10:35

❧ Contentment ❧

The boundary lines have fallen for me in
pleasant places; surely I have a delightful
inheritance.

—PSALM 16:6 (NIV)

I will be *fully satisfied* when I awake [to find
myself] beholding God's form [and having
sweet communion with Him].

—PSALM 17:15

A day in Your courts is better than a thousand
[anywhere else]; I would rather be a
doorkeeper and stand at the threshold in the
house of my God than to dwell [at ease] in
the tents of wickedness.

—PSALM 84:10

You make me glad by your deeds, O Lord; I
sing for joy at the works of your hands. How

great are your works, O Lord, how profound your thoughts!

—PSALM 92:4-5 (NIV)

I give thanks to the Lord for his unfailing love and his wonderful deeds for me, for he satisfies the thirsty and fills the hungry with good things.

—PSALM 107:8-9 (NIV)

It's healthy to be content, but envy can eat me up.

—PROVERBS 14:30 (CEV)

Jesus is the Bread of Life. I come to Him and I am never hungry. I believe in Him, cleave to, trust in and rely on Him. I am never thirsty at any time. I am fully satisfied.

—JOHN 6:35

I'm glad in God, far happier than you would ever guess. I don't have a sense of needing anything personally. I've learned by now to be quite content whatever my circumstances.

—PHILIPPIANS 4:10-11 (THE MESSAGE)

God meets all my needs according to His riches in glory by Christ Jesus.

—PHILIPPIANS 4:19

[It is, indeed, a source of immense profit, for] godliness accompanied with contentment (that contentment which is a sense of inward sufficiency) is great and abundant gain. For I brought nothing into the world, and obviously I cannot take anything out of the world; but if I have food and clothing, with these I shall be content (satisfied).

—1 TIMOTHY 6:6-8

I keep my life free from the love of money and I am content with what I have, because God has said, "Never will I leave you; never will I forsake you." So I say with confidence, "The Lord is my helper; I will not be afraid. What can man do to me?"

—HEBREWS 13:5-6 (NIV)

✢ Control ✢

I am a God-pleaser, not a people-pleaser. I
obey God before man.

—ACTS 5:29

I am living the life of the Spirit because the
Holy Spirit dwells within me [directs and
controls me].

—ROMANS 8:9

I am not controlled by what people think of
me. As long as God is satisfied with me I am
satisfied.

—1 CORINTHIANS 4:3-4

The love of Christ controls me.

—2 CORINTHIANS 5:14

I don't try to be popular with people. All I
want is to do the will of God.

—GALATIANS 1:10

I love people and I want them to be happy
with me but I don't allow them to control
me. I am led by the Holy Spirit.
—COLOSSIANS 1:10 & 1 THESSALONIANS 2:4

✦ Courage ✦

I am strong and of good courage, I do not fear
nor am I afraid, for the Lord my God, He is
the one who goes with me. He will not leave
me nor forsake me.

—DEUTERONOMY 31:6 (NKJV)

I am strong, vigorous, and very courageous.
I am not afraid, neither am I dismayed, for
the Lord my God is with me wherever I go.

—JOSHUA 1:9

I am strong and courageous. I am not afraid
or discouraged, because the Lord my God is
with me to help me fight my battles.

—2 CHRONICLES 32:7-8 (NIV)

As I wait on the Lord, with good courage,
He shall strengthen my heart.

—PSALM 27:14 (NKJV)

I am strong and my heart takes courage, for I
wait for and hope for and expect the Lord!

—PSALM 31:24

He spoke to them, saying, Take courage!
I AM! Stop being afraid!

—MATTHEW 14:27

I am standing firm, letting nothing move me.
I give myself fully to the work of the Lord,
because I know that my labor in the Lord is
not in vain.

—1 CORINTHIANS 15:58 (NIV)

I am alert and on my guard; standing firm in
my faith (my conviction respecting my relationship to God and divine things, keeping
the trust and holy fervor born of faith and a
part of it). I am courageous; growing in
strength!

—1 CORINTHIANS 16:13

I have courage in God's presence, because I am sure that he hears me if I ask him for anything that is according to his will.

—1 JOHN 5:14 (GNT)

☙ Depression ❧

The Lord goes before me; He will [march] with me; He will not fail me or let me go or forsake me; I will fear not, neither become broken [in spirit—depressed, dismayed, and unnerved with alarm].

—DEUTERONOMY 31:8

God is my shield, my glory and the lifter of my head.

—PSALM 3:3

The eyes of the Lord are on me, and His ears are open to my cry. . . . When I cry out, the Lord hears, and delivers me out of all my troubles.

—PSALM 34:15, 17 (NKJV)

I WAITED patiently and expectantly for the Lord; and He inclined to me and heard my cry. He drew me up out of a horrible pit [a pit of tumult and of destruction], out of the miry clay (froth and slime), and set my feet upon a rock, steadying my steps and establishing my goings. And He has put a new song in my mouth, a song of praise to our God.

—PSALM 40:1-3

Why are you down in the dumps, dear soul? Why are you crying the blues? I fix my eyes on God and soon I'll be praising again. He puts a smile on my face. He's my God.

—PSALM 42:5 (THE MESSAGE)

When my soul is cast down within me I remember the Lord and His goodness to me. . . . He commands His loving-kindness in the daytime, and in the night His song shall be with me—a prayer to the God of my life. . . . I say to myself, "Why are you cast down, O my soul? And why are you disquieted within me? I hope in God; for I shall yet praise Him, the help of my countenance and my God."

—PSALM 42:6, 8, 11 (NKJV)

I will cry to God with my voice, and He will give ear and hearken to me. In the day of my trouble I seek (inquire of and desperately require) the Lord.

—PSALM 77:1-2

Because I have set my love upon the Lord, He will deliver me; He will set me on high, because I know and understand His name [I have a personal knowledge of His mercy, love, and kindness—I trust and rely on Him, knowing that He will never forsake me, no, never]. I shall call upon Him, and He will answer me; He will be with me in trouble, He will deliver me and honor me. With long life

will [the Lord] satisfy me and show me His
salvation.

—PSALM 91:14-16

I fear not, for I shall not be ashamed; neither
will I be confounded and depressed, for I shall
not be put to shame.

—ISAIAH 54:4

I ARISE [from the depression and prostration
in which circumstances have kept me—I arise
to a new life]! I shine [am radiant with the
glory of the Lord), for my light has come, and
the glory of the Lord has risen upon me!

—ISAIAH 60:1

But God, Who comforts and encourages and
refreshes and cheers the depressed and the
sinking, comforted and encouraged and
refreshed and cheered me.

—2 CORINTHIANS 7:6

I humble myself under the mighty hand of
God, that He may exalt me in due time . . .
casting all my care upon Him, for He cares
for me.

—1 PETER 5:6, 7 (NKJV)

☙ Determination ❧

I wait for the Lord [I expect, look for, and hope in Him]. I shall change and renew my strength and power. I shall lift my wings and mount up [close to God] as eagles [mount up to the sun]; I shall (am determined to) run and not be weary, I shall walk and not faint or become tired.

—ISAIAH 40:31

For I determined not to know anything except Jesus Christ and Him crucified.

—1 CORINTHIANS 2:2 (NKJV)

I set my mind and keep it set on what is above (the higher things), not on the things that are on the earth.

—COLOSSIANS 3:2

I make it my ambition and definitely endeavor to live quietly and peacefully, to mind my own affairs, and to work with my hands. So that I may bear myself becomingly and be correct and honorable and command the respect of the outside world, being dependent on nobody [self-supporting] and having need of nothing.

—1 THESSALONIANS 4:11-12

I aim at and pursue righteousness (right standing with God and true goodness), godliness (which is the loving fear of God and being Christlike), faith, love, steadfastness (patience), and gentleness of heart. I fight the good fight of the faith; lay hold of the eternal life to which I was summoned and [for which] I confessed the good confession [of faith] before many witnesses. I determine to keep all the precepts of the Lord unsullied and flawless, irreproachable, until the appearing of our Lord Jesus Christ (the Anointed One).

—1 TIMOTHY 6:11-14

I withstand [the enemy]; I am firm in faith
[against his onset—rooted, established,
strong, immovable, and determined],
knowing that the same (identical) sufferings
are appointed to my brotherhood (the whole
body of Christians) throughout the world.

—1 PETER 5:9

☩ Diligence ☩

If I diligently hearken to the voice of the Lord my God and do what is right in His sight, and listen to and obey His commandments and keep all His statutes, God will put none of the diseases upon me which He brought upon the Egyptians, for He is the Lord Who heals me.

—EXODUS 15:26

I take heed, and guard my life diligently, lest I forget the things which my eyes have seen and lest they depart from my [mind and] heart all the days of my life. I teach them to my children and my children's children.

—DEUTERONOMY 4:9

The Lord has commanded me to keep His precepts, that I should observe them diligently.

—PSALM 119:4

I keep my heart with all diligence, for out of it spring the issues of life.

—PROVERBS 4:23 (NKJV)

The Lord loves those who love Him, and those who seek Him early and diligently shall find Him.

—PROVERBS 8:17

He becomes poor who works with a slack and idle hand, but the hand of the diligent makes rich.

—PROVERBS 10:4

The hand of the diligent will rule, but the slothful will be put to forced labor.

—PROVERBS 12:24

The appetite of the sluggard craves and gets nothing, but the appetite of the diligent is abundantly supplied.

—PROVERBS 13:4

The thoughts of the [steadily] diligent tend only to plenteousness, but everyone who is impatient and hasty hastens only to want.

—PROVERBS 21:5

Without faith it is impossible to please and be satisfactory to God. For whoever would come near to God must [necessarily] believe that God exists and that He is the rewarder of those who earnestly and diligently seek Him [out].

—HEBREWS 11:6

✢ Discouragement and Despair ✢

You, O Lord, are a shield for me, my glory, and the lifter of my head.

—PSALM 3:3

You have turned my mourning into joyful dancing. You have taken away my clothes of mourning and clothed me with joy, that I might sing praises to you and not be silent. O Lord my God, I will give you thanks forever.

—PSALM 30:11-12 (NLT)

The thief comes only in order to steal and kill and destroy. But Jesus came that I may have and enjoy life, and have it in abundance (to the full, till it overflows).

—JOHN 10:10

In Christ I have [perfect] peace and confidence. In the world I have tribulation and

trials and distress and frustration; but I can be
of good cheer [take courage; be confident,
certain, undaunted]! For Christ has overcome
the world. [He has deprived it of power to
harm me and has conquered it for me.]

—JOHN 16:33

I am assured and know that [God being a
partner in my labor] all things work together
and are [fitting into a plan] for good to and for
me because I love God and I am called
according to [His] design and purpose.

—ROMANS 8:28

God comforts, encourages and consoles me in
every trouble. He enables me to console
others who need comfort.

—2 CORINTHIANS 1:4

When I am pressed on every side by troubles,
I am not crushed and broken. When I am

perplexed because I don't know why things happen as they do, I don't give up and quit.

—2 CORINTHIANS 4:8 (TLB)

I do not become discouraged (utterly spiritless, exhausted, and wearied out through fear). Though my outer man is [progressively] decaying and wasting away, yet my inner self is being [progressively] renewed day after day. For my light, momentary affliction (this slight distress of the passing hour) is ever more and more abundantly preparing and producing and achieving for me an everlasting weight of glory [beyond all measure, excessively surpassing all comparisons and all calculations, a vast and transcendent glory and blessedness never to cease!].

—2 CORINTHIANS 4:16-17

God's gracious favor is all I need. His power
works best in my weakness.

—2 CORINTHIANS 12:9 (NLT)

I have strength for all things in Christ Who
empowers me [I am ready for anything and
equal to anything through Him Who infuses
inner strength into me; I am self-sufficient in
Christ's sufficiency].

—PHILIPPIANS 4:13

⚜ Emotions ⚜

You establish me, O God, and all the
[uncompromisingly] righteous [those upright
and in harmony with You]; for You, Who try
the hearts and emotions and thinking powers,
are a righteous God.

—PSALM 7:9

Weeping may endure for a night, but joy
comes in the morning.

—PSALM 30:5

If my heart is broken, I'll find God right there;
if I'm kicked in the gut, He'll help me catch
my breath.

—PSALM 34:18 (THE MESSAGE)

Why are you cast down, O my inner self?
And why should you moan over me and be
disquieted within me? My hope is in God

and I wait expectantly for Him, for I shall yet praise Him, my Help and my God.

—PSALM 42:5

God makes me to hear joy and gladness and be satisfied. He restores to me the joy of His salvation and upholds me with a willing spirit.

—PSALM 51:8, 12

God gives me the power to keep myself calm in the days of adversity, until the [inevitable] pit of corruption is dug for the wicked.

—PSALM 94:13

When I feel hurt or brokenhearted God binds up my wounds and cures my pain and sorrow.

—PSALM 147:3

I walk in the Spirit, I don't cater to the impulses of my carnal nature.

—ROMANS 8:8

I am learning how to be content (satisfied to the point where I am not disturbed or disquieted) in whatever state I am.

—PHILIPPIANS 4:11

My High Priest is not one who cannot feel sympathy for my weaknesses. On the contrary, I have a High Priest who was tempted in every way that I am, but did not sin. So I have confidence, then, and approach God's throne, where there is grace. There I will receive mercy and find grace to help me just when I need it.

—HEBREWS 4:15-16 (GNT)

I am rooted, established, strong, immovable, and determined.

—1 PETER 5:9

❧ Encouragement and Comfort ❧

In the day of trouble He will hide me in His
shelter; in the secret place of His tent will He
hide me; He will set me high upon a rock.

—PSALM 27:5

I am overcome with joy because of God's
unfailing love, for He has seen my troubles,
and He cares about the anguish of my soul.

—PSALM 31:7 (NLT)

I call out to High God, the God who holds me
together. He sends orders from heaven and
saves me. God delivers generous love, he
makes good on his word.

—PSALM 57:2-3 (THE MESSAGE)

FOR GOD alone my soul waits in silence;
from Him comes my salvation. He only is my

Rock and my Salvation, my Defense and my Fortress, I shall not be greatly moved.

—PSALM 62:1-2

This is my comfort and consolation in my affliction: that Your word has revived me and given me life.

—PSALM 119:50

Though I am surrounded by troubles, my God will preserve me against the anger of my enemies. He will clench his fist against my angry enemies! His power will save me. The Lord will work out his plans for my life—for his faithful love endures forever.

—PSALM 138:7-8 (NLT)

Blessed be the God and Father of our Lord Jesus Christ, the Father of sympathy (pity and mercy) and the God [Who is the Source] of every comfort (consolation and encouragement), Who comforts (consoles and encourages) me in every trouble (calamity and affliction), so that I may also be able to comfort (console and encourage) those who are in any kind of trouble or distress, with the comfort (consolation and encouragement) with which I myself am comforted (consoled and encouraged) by God.

—2 CORINTHIANS 1:3-4

And this small and temporary trouble I suffer will bring me a tremendous and eternal glory, much greater than the trouble. For I fix my attention, not on things that are seen, but on things that are unseen. What can be seen lasts only for a time, but what cannot be seen lasts forever.

—2 CORINTHIANS 4:17-18 (GNT)

Our Lord Jesus Christ Himself and God our Father, Who loved us and gave us everlasting consolation and encouragement and well-founded hope through [His] grace (unmerited favor), comforts and encourages my heart and strengthens me [makes me steadfast and keeps me unswerving] in every good work and word.

—2 THESSALONIANS 2:16-17

☙ Faith ❧

I am a just person. I shall live by my faith.

—HABAKKUK 2:4 (NKJV)

If I have faith [that is living] like a grain of
mustard seed, I can say to this mountain,
Move from here to yonder place, and it will
move; and nothing will be impossible to me.

—MATTHEW 17:20

Whoever says to this mountain, be lifted up
and thrown into the sea and does not doubt
at all in his heart but believes that what he
says will take place, it will be done for him.

—MARK 11:23

I am justified and made upright by faith
independent of and distinctly apart from
good deeds (works of the Law).

—ROMANS 3:28

Through Him also I have [my] access (entrance, introduction) by faith into this grace (state of God's favor) in which I [firmly and safely] stand. And I rejoice and exult in my hope of experiencing and enjoying the glory of God.

—ROMANS 5:2

Faith comes from listening to this message of good news—the Good News about Christ.

—ROMANS 10:17 (NLT)

Whatever is not of faith is sin.

—ROMANS 14:23

May God, the source of hope, fill me with all joy and peace by means of my faith in him, so that my hope will continue to grow by the power of the Holy Spirit.

—ROMANS 15:13 (GNT)

My faith does not rest in the wisdom of men (human philosophy), but in the power of God.

—1 CORINTHIANS 2:5

I live by faith, not by sight.

—2 CORINTHIANS 5:7 (NIV)

The law was put in charge to lead me to Christ that I might be justified by faith. Now that faith has come, I am no longer under the supervision of the law.

—GALATIANS 3:24-25 (NIV)

Because of my faith in Him, I dare to have the boldness (courage and confidence) of free access (an unreserved approach to God with freedom and without fear).

—EPHESIANS 3:12

I lift up over all the [covering] shield of saving
faith, upon which I can quench all the flaming
missiles of the wicked [one].

—EPHESIANS 6:16

I fight the good fight of faith, laying hold of
the eternal life to which I was summoned and
[for which] I confessed the good confession
[of faith] before many witnesses.

—1 TIMOTHY 6:12

I draw near with a true heart in full assurance
of faith, having my heart sprinkled from an
evil conscience and my body washed with
pure water. I hold fast the confession of my
hope without wavering, for He who
promised is faithful.

—HEBREWS 10:22-23 (NKJV)

Faith is being sure of what I hope for and
certain of what I do not see. . . . By faith I
understand that the universe was formed at

God's command, so that what is seen was not
made out of what was visible.

—HEBREWS 11:1, 3 (NIV)

Without faith it is impossible to please God
and those who come to Him must believe
that He is, and that He is a rewarder of those
who diligently seek Him.

—HEBREWS 11:6 (NKJV)

Faith, if it does not have works (deeds and
actions of obedience to back it up), by itself is
destitute of power (inoperative, dead).

—JAMES 2:17

⅌ Favor ⅌

You have granted me life and favor, and Your
providence has preserved my spirit.

—JOB 10:12

You, Lord, will bless me and all the [uncom-
promisingly] righteous [all who are upright
and in right standing with You]; as with a
shield You will surround me with goodwill
(pleasure and favor).

—PSALM 5:12

By Your favor, O Lord, You have established
me as a strong mountain.

—PSALM 30:7

You are the glory of my strength [my proud
adornment], and by Your favor my horn is
exalted and I walk with uplifted face!

—PSALM 89:17

I shall find favor, good understanding, and
high esteem in the sight [or judgment] of God
and man.

—PROVERBS 3:4

I who diligently seek good seek [God's] favor,
but he who searches after evil, it shall come
upon him.

—PROVERBS 11:27

I obtain favor from the Lord, but a man of
wicked devices God condemns.

—PROVERBS 12:2

Fools make a mock of sin and sin mocks the
fools [bringing them disappointment and
disfavor], but because I am among the
upright, I have the favor of God.

—PROVERBS 14:9

Blessed and enviably happy [with a happiness
produced by the experience of God's favor

and especially conditioned by the revelation
of His matchless grace] are those who mourn,
for they shall be comforted!

—MATTHEW 5:4

God's grace (His favor and loving-kindness
and mercy) is enough for me [sufficient
against any danger and enables me to bear
the trouble manfully]; for God's strength and
power are made perfect (fulfilled and
completed) and show themselves most
effective in [my] weakness. Therefore, I will
all the more gladly glory in my weaknesses
and infirmities, that the strength and power
of Christ (the Messiah) may rest (yes, may
pitch a tent over and dwell) upon me!

—2 CORINTHIANS 12:9

He Who raised up the Lord Jesus will raise me
up also with Jesus and bring me [along] into
His presence. For all [these] things are [taking
place] for my sake, so that the more grace

(divine favor and spiritual blessing) extends
to more and more people and multiplies
through the many, the more thanksgiving
may increase [and redound] to the glory of
God.

—2 CORINTHIANS 4:14-15

God is so rich in mercy, and he loved me
so very much, that even while I was dead
because of my sins, he gave me life when he
raised Christ from the dead. (It is only by
God's special favor that I have been saved!)
For he raised me from the dead along with
Christ, and I am seated with him in the
heavenly realms—all because I am one with
Christ Jesus. And so God can always point to
me as an example of the incredible wealth of
his favor and kindness toward me, as shown
in all he has done for me through Christ
Jesus.

—EPHESIANS 2:4-7 (NLT)

I fearlessly and confidently and boldly draw
near to the throne of grace (the throne of
God's unmerited favor to us sinners), that I
may receive mercy [for my failures] and find
grace to help in good time for every need
[appropriate help and well-timed help,
coming just when I need it].

—HEBREWS 4:16

❧ Fear ❧

Yes, though I walk through the [deep, sunless] valley of the shadow of death, I will fear or dread no evil, for You are with me; Your rod [to protect] and Your staff [to guide], they comfort me.

—PSALM 23:4

THE LORD is my Light and my Salvation—whom shall I fear or dread? The Lord is the Refuge and Stronghold of my life—of whom shall I be afraid?

—PSALM 27:1

God will cover me with his wings; I will be safe in his care; his faithfulness will protect and defend me. I need not fear any dangers at night or sudden attacks during the day.

—PSALM 91:4-5 (GNT)

I am not afraid of receiving bad news; my faith is strong, and I trust in the Lord. I am not worried or afraid.

—PSALM 112:7-8 (GNT)

The fear of man brings a snare, but because I lean on, trust in, and put my confidence in the Lord, I am safe and set on high.

—PROVERBS 29:25

I fear not [there is nothing to fear], for God is with me. I do not look around in terror and be dismayed, for He is my God. He will strengthen and harden me to difficulties, yes, God will help me; yes, He will hold me up and retain me with His [victorious] right hand of rightness and justice.

—ISAIAH 41:10

In righteousness I will be established: Tyranny will be far from me; I will have

nothing to fear. Terror will be far removed; it
will not come near me.

—ISAIAH 54:14 (NIV)

I will not be seized with alarm and struck
with fear, for it is my Father's good pleasure
to give me the kingdom!

—LUKE 12:32

God has not given me a spirit of fear and
timidity, but of power, love, and self-
discipline.

—2 TIMOTHY 1:7 (NLT)

[God] Himself has said, He will not in any
way fail me nor give me up nor leave me
without support. [He will] not, [He will] not,
[He will] not in any degree leave me helpless
nor forsake nor let [me] down (relax His hold
on me)! [Assuredly not!] So I take comfort
and am encouraged and confidently and
boldly say, The Lord is my Helper; I will not

be seized with alarm [I will not fear or dread or be terrified]. What can man do to me?

—HEBREWS 13:5-6

Even if I suffer for doing what is right, God will reward me for it. So I won't be afraid or worry.

—1 PETER 3:14 (NLT)

There is no fear in love [dread does not exist], but full-grown (complete, perfect) love turns fear out of doors and expels every trace of terror!

—1 JOHN 4:18

⚜ Forgiveness ⚜

The Lord my God is gracious and merciful,
and He will not turn away His face from me
if I return to Him.

—2 CHRONICLES 30:9 (NKJV)

If I forgive people their trespasses [their
reckless and willful sins, leaving them, letting
them go, and giving up resentment], my
heavenly Father will also forgive me.

—MATTHEW 6:14

And whenever I stand praying, if I have
anything against anyone, I forgive him and let
it drop (leave it, let it go), in order that my
Father Who is in heaven may also forgive me
my [own] failings and shortcomings and let
them drop. But if I do not forgive, neither will
my Father in heaven forgive my failings and
shortcomings.

—MARK 11:25-26

I condemn not, and I shall not be condemned.
I forgive, and I will be forgiven.

—LUKE 6:37 (NKJV)

I am blessed and happy and to be envied
because my iniquities are forgiven and my
sins are covered up and completely buried.
The Lord will take no account nor reckon it
against me.

—ROMANS 4:7-8

I am useful and helpful and kind to others,
tenderhearted (compassionate, understanding, loving-hearted), forgiving others [readily
and freely], as God in Christ forgave me.

—EPHESIANS 4:32

I am gentle and forbearing with others and,
if someone has a difference (a grievance or
complaint) against me, I readily pardon him;
even as the Lord has [freely] forgiven me, so
must I also [forgive].

—COLOSSIANS 3:13

Believing-prayer will heal me, and Jesus will put me on my feet. And if I've sinned, I'll be forgiven—healed inside and out.

—JAMES 5:15 (THE MESSAGE)

If we confess our sins, He is faithful and just to forgive us our sins and to cleanse us from all unrighteousness. If we say that we have not sinned, we make Him a liar, and His word is not in us.

—1 JOHN 1:9-10 (NKJV)

For His name's sake my sins are forgiven [pardoned through His name and on account of confessing His name].

—1 JOHN 2:12

ⵈ Grace ⵈ

The Lord God is a Sun and Shield; the Lord
bestows [present] grace and favor and [future]
glory (honor, splendor, and heavenly bliss)!
No good thing will He withhold from me,
because I walk uprightly.

—PSALM 84:11

I am growing and becoming strong in spirit,
filled with wisdom; and the grace (favor and
spiritual blessing) of God is upon me.

—LUKE 2:40

I [trust myself to and stand fast] in the grace
(the unmerited favor and blessing) of God.

—ACTS 13:43

[I] am justified and made upright and in right
standing with God, freely and gratuitously by
His grace (His unmerited favor and mercy),

through the redemption which is [provided] in Christ Jesus.

—ROMANS 3:24

In no way do I compare God's free gift to the trespass [His grace is out of all proportion to the fall of man]. For if many died through my falling away (my lapse, my offense), much more profusely did God's grace and the free gift [that comes] through the undeserved favor of the one Man Jesus Christ abound and overflow to and for [the benefit of] many.

—ROMANS 5:15

Where sin abounds, grace abounds much more, so that as sin reigns in death, even so grace might reign through righteousness to eternal life through Jesus Christ our Lord.

—ROMANS 5:20-21 (NKJV)

I am God's fellow worker; I am God's field, God's building. By the grace God has given me, I laid a foundation as an expert builder, and someone else is building on it. But each one should be careful how he builds. For no one can lay any foundation other than the one already laid, which is Jesus Christ.

—1 CORINTHIANS 3:9-11 (NIV)

It is by free grace (God's unmerited favor) that I am saved (delivered from judgment and made a partaker of Christ's salvation) through [my] faith. And this [salvation] is not of myself [of my own doing, it came not through my own striving], but it is the gift of God.

—EPHESIANS 2:8

He [God] gives me more and more grace (power of the Holy Spirit, to meet this evil tendency and all others fully). That is why He says, God sets Himself against the proud and haughty, but gives grace [continually] to the lowly (those who are humble enough to receive it).

—JAMES 4:6

✛ Guilt and Condemnation ✛

I am ever [on guard] to keep myself free from my sin and guilt.

—PSALM 18:23

God has mercy upon me, according to His lovingkindness; according to the multitude of His tender mercies, He blots out my transgressions. He washes me thoroughly from my iniquity, and cleanses me from my sin.

—PSALM 51:1-2 (NKJV)

Wash me, and I shall [in reality] be whiter than snow. God makes me to hear joy and gladness and I am satisfied. God hides His face from my sins and blots out all my guilt and iniquities.

—PSALM 51:7-9

He was wounded for my transgressions, He was bruised for my guilt and iniquities; the

chastisement [needful to obtain] peace and
well-being for me was upon Him, and with
the stripes [that wounded] Him I am healed
and made whole.

—ISAIAH 53:5

No one understands [no one intelligently
discerns or comprehends]; no one seeks out
God. All have turned aside; together they
have gone wrong and have become
unprofitable and worthless; no one does
right, not even one! . . . But now the
righteousness of God has been revealed,
namely, the righteousness of God which
comes by believing with personal trust and
confident reliance on Jesus Christ (the
Messiah). [And it is meant] for all who
believe. It is meant for me.

—ROMANS 3:11-12, 21-22

There is therefore now no condemnation to
those who are in Christ Jesus. I am in Christ

Jesus. I do not walk according to the flesh, but according to the Spirit. For the law of the Spirit of life in Christ Jesus has made me free from the law of sin and death.

—ROMANS 8:1-2 (NKJV)

Because Christ lives in me, [then although] my [natural] body is dead by reason of sin and guilt, the spirit is alive because of [the] righteousness [that He imputes to me].

—ROMANS 8:10

God does not condemn me because He has justified me, Jesus does not condemn me because He is seated at the right hand of God pleading for me in intercession.

—ROMANS 8:33-34

According to God's word I have been made the righteousness of God in Christ.

—2 CORINTHIANS 5:21 (KJV)

God [the Light-being, the out-raying or radiance of the divine], accomplished my cleansing of sins and riddance of guilt.

—HEBREWS 1:3

I draw near to God with a sincere heart in full assurance of faith, having my heart sprinkled to cleanse me from a guilty conscience and having my body washed with pure water. I will hold unswervingly to the hope I profess, for he who promised is faithful.

—HEBREWS 10:22-23 (NIV)

I do not love with words or tongue but with actions and in truth. This then is how I know that I belong to the truth, and how I set my heart at rest in his presence whenever my heart condemns me. For God is greater than my heart, and he knows everything.

—1 JOHN 3:18-20 (NIV)

☀ Health and Healing ☀

I cry out to the Lord and He heals me.
—PSALM 30:2

The Lord forgives all my sins and heals all my diseases.
—PSALM 103:3 (NIV)

He sends His word and heals me and rescues me from the pit and destruction.
—PSALM 107:20

I shall not die but live, and shall declare the works and recount the illustrious acts of the Lord.
—PSALM 118:17

He heals my broken heart and binds up my wounds [curing my pains and sorrows].
—PSALM 147:3

I will listen closely to God's words. I will not let them out of my sight—I will keep them within my heart; for they are life to all who find them and health for the whole body.

—PROVERBS 4:20-22 (NIV)

My light shall break forth like the morning, and my healing (my restoration and the power of a new life) shall spring forth speedily.

—ISAIAH 58:8

Heal me, O Lord, and I shall be healed; save me, and I shall be saved, for You are my praise.

—JEREMIAH 17:14

The Lord has declared that He will restore me to health and heal my wounds.

—JEREMIAH 30:17 (NIV)

When I am sick, I will call the elders of the church to pray over me and anoint me with oil in the name of the Lord. And the prayer offered in faith will make me well; the Lord will raise me up.

—JAMES 5:14-15 (NIV)

He Himself bore my sins in his body on the tree, so that I might die to sins and live for righteousness; by his wounds I have been healed.

—1 PETER 2:24 (NIV)

I pray that I may enjoy good health and that all may go well with me, even as my soul is getting along well.

—3 JOHN 2 (NIV)

⚜ Hearing from God ⚜

Because I listen diligently to the voice of the Lord my God, being watchful to do all His commandments which He commands me this day, the Lord my God will set me high above all the nations of the earth.

—DEUTERONOMY 28:1

God has given me the capacity to hear and obey [His law, a more valuable service than] burnt offerings and sin offerings [which] He does not require.

—PSALM 40:6

Today I will hear His voice . . . and harden not my heart.

—PSALM 95:7, 8

Your statutes are wonderful; therefore I obey them. The unfolding of your words gives light; it gives understanding to the simple.

—PSALM 119:129-130 (NIV)

Because I listen to and obey God's voice, He will be my God and I will be one of His people.

—JEREMIAH 7:23

I hear the words of the Lord and act upon them [obeying them] like a sensible (prudent, practical, wise) man who built his house upon the rock. And the rain fell and the floods came and the winds blew and beat against that house; yet it did not fall, because it had been founded on the rock.

—MATTHEW 7:24-25

As I hear the Word of the kingdom (sown in the good soil of my heart), and grasp and

comprehend it; . . . it will indeed bear fruit
and yield a good return.

—MATTHEW 13:19, 23

I hear my Father's voice and the voice of a
stranger I will not follow.

—JOHN 10:5

I am one of God's sheep and His sheep hear
His voice.

—JOHN 10:27

Faith comes by hearing, and hearing by the
word of God.

—ROMANS 10:17 (NKJV)

I do not merely listen to the word, and so
deceive myself. I do what it says. Anyone
who listens to the word but does not do what
it says is like a man who looks at his face in a
mirror and, after looking at himself, goes
away and immediately forgets what he looks

like. But the man who looks intently into the perfect law that gives freedom, and continues to do this, not forgetting what he has heard, but doing it—he will be blessed in what he does.

—JAMES 1:22-25 (NIV)

☘ Help ☘

The Lord is my Strength and my [impenetrable] Shield; my heart trusts in, relies on, and confidently leans on Him, and I am helped; therefore my heart greatly rejoices, and with my song will I praise Him.

—PSALM 28:7

The eyes of the Lord are toward the [uncompromisingly] righteous and His ears are open to my cry. . . . When I cry for help, the Lord hears, and delivers me out of all my distress and troubles.

—PSALM 34:15, 17

When I call on God in the day of trouble; He will deliver me, and I will honor and glorify Him.

—PSALM 50:15

I leave my troubles with the Lord, and He will defend me; He never lets honest people be defeated.

—PSALM 55:22 (GNT)

Unless the Lord had been my help, I would soon have dwelt in [the land where there is] silence. When I said, My foot is slipping, Your mercy and loving-kindness, O Lord, held me up. In the multitude of my [anxious] thoughts within me, Your comforts cheer and delight my soul!

—PSALM 94:17-19

You are my God; teach me to do your will. Be good to me, and guide me on a safe path. Rescue me, Lord, as you have promised; in your goodness save me from my troubles!

—PSALM 143:10-11 (GNT)

The Lord my God holds my right hand; He is the Lord, Who says to me, Fear not; I will help you!

—ISAIAH 41:13

Because the Lord God helps me, I will not be dismayed; therefore, I have set my face like flint to do his will, and I know that I will triumph.

—ISAIAH 50:7 (TLB)

The Lord is good, a Strength and Stronghold in my day of trouble; He knows (recognizes, has knowledge of, and understands) those who take refuge and trust in Him.

—NAHUM 1:7

I take comfort and am encouraged and confidently and boldly say, The Lord is my Helper; I will not be seized with alarm [I will not fear or dread or be terrified].

—HEBREWS 13:6

✢ Holiness ✢

I consecrate myself therefore, and I will be holy; for He is the Lord my God.

—LEVITICUS 20:7

I always exercise and discipline myself [mortifying my body, deadening my carnal affections, bodily appetites, and worldly desires, endeavoring in all respects] to have a clear (unshaken, blameless) conscience, void of offense toward God and toward men.

—ACTS 24:16

According to God's word I have been set free from sin and have become the slave of God, I have my present reward in holiness and its end is eternal life.

—ROMANS 6:22

I have made a decisive dedication of my body [presenting all my members and faculties] as a

living sacrifice, holy (devoted, consecrated) and well pleasing to God, which is my reasonable (rational, intelligent) service and spiritual worship. I am not conformed to this world (this age), [fashioned after and adapted to its external, superficial customs], but I am transformed (changed) by the [entire] renewal of my mind [by its new ideals and its new attitude], so that I may prove [for myself] what is the good and acceptable and perfect will of God, even the thing which is good and acceptable and perfect [in His sight for me].
—ROMANS 12:1-2

My body is the temple (the very sanctuary) of the Holy Spirit Who lives within me, Whom I have received [as a Gift] from God. I am not my own, I was bought with a price [purchased with a preciousness and paid for, made His own]. So then, I honor God and bring glory to Him in my body.
—1 CORINTHIANS 6:19-20

[In His love] He chose me [actually picked me out for Himself as His own] in Christ before the foundation of the world, that I should be holy (consecrated and set apart for Him) and blameless in His sight, even above reproach, before Him in love.

—EPHESIANS 1:4

I am constantly renewed in the spirit of my mind [having a fresh mental and spiritual attitude], and I put on the new nature (the regenerate self) created in God's image, [Godlike] in true righteousness and holiness.

—EPHESIANS 4:23-24

God has reconciled me by Christ's physical body through death to present me holy in his sight, without blemish and free from accusation.

—COLOSSIANS 1:22 (NIV)

I strive to live in peace with everybody and pursue that consecration and holiness without which no one will [ever] see the Lord.

—HEBREWS 12:14

God disciplines me for my certain good that I might become a partaker of His holiness.

—HEBREWS 12:10

I live in obedience [to God]; I do not conform myself to the evil desires [that governed me] in my former ignorance [when I did not know the requirements of the gospel]. The One Who called me is holy and I am also holy in all my conduct and manner of living.

—1 PETER 1:14-15

⊰ Hope ⊱

The Lord's eye is upon me because I fear Him
[I revere and worship Him with awe], I wait
for Him and hope in His mercy and loving-
kindness.

—PSALM 33:18

The Lord takes pleasure in me and all who
reverently and worshipfully fear Him, in
those who hope in His mercy and loving-
kindness.

—PSALM 147:11

Hope deferred makes my heart sick, but
when my desire is fulfilled, it is a tree of life.

—PROVERBS 13:12

I'm sticking with God. I say it over and over
again—He's all I've got left. He proves to be
good to me and to all who passionately wait

and diligently seek Him. It's a good thing to quietly hope for help from God.

—LAMENTATIONS 3:24-26 (THE MESSAGE)

I rejoice and exult in hope; I'm steadfast and patient in suffering and tribulation; constant in prayer.

—ROMANS 12:12

Everything that was written in the past was written to teach me, so that through endurance and the encouragement of the Scriptures I might have hope.

—ROMANS 15:4 (NIV)

May the God of my hope so fill me with all joy and peace in believing [through the experience of my faith] that by the power of the Holy Spirit I may abound and be overflowing (bubbling over) with hope.

—ROMANS 15:13

When the Complete arrives, my incompletes will be canceled. I don't yet see things clearly. I'm squinting in a fog, peering through a mist. But it won't be long before the weather clears and the sun shines bright! I'll see it all then, see it all as clearly as God sees me, knowing him directly just as he knows me! But for right now, until that completeness, I have three things to do to lead me toward that consummation: Trust steadily in God, hope unswervingly, love extravagantly. And the best of the three is love.

—1 CORINTHIANS 13:10, 12-13 (THE MESSAGE)

I shall be changed (transformed) in a moment, in the twinkling of an eye, at the [sound of the] last trumpet call. For a trumpet will sound, and the dead [in Christ] will be raised imperishable (free and immune from decay), and I shall be changed (transformed). . . . And when this perishable puts on the imperish-

able and this that was capable of dying puts
on freedom from death, then shall be fulfilled
the Scripture that says, Death is swallowed
up (utterly vanquished forever) in and unto
victory.

—1 CORINTHIANS 15:51-52, 54

By having the eyes of my heart flooded with
light, I can know and understand the hope to
which He has called me, and how rich is His
glorious inheritance in the saints (His set-
apart ones).

—EPHESIANS 1:18

I brace up my mind and am sober (circum-
spect, morally alert) setting my hope wholly
and unchangeably on the grace (divine favor)
that is coming to me when Jesus Christ (the
Messiah) is revealed.

—1 PETER 1:13

❧ Humility and Pride ❧

He leads the humble in what is right, and the humble He teaches His way.

—PSALM 25:9

I am humble and the humble will see their God at work and be glad. Let all who seek God's help live in joy.

—PSALM 69:32 (NLT)

The Lord lifts up the humble and downtrodden; He casts the wicked down to the ground.

—PSALM 147:6

When swelling and pride come, then emptiness and shame come also, but with the humble (those who are lowly, who have been pruned or chiseled by trial, and renounce self) are skillful and godly Wisdom and soundness.

—PROVERBS 11:2

Fear of the Lord teaches a person to be wise;
humility precedes honor.

—PROVERBS 15:33 (NLT)

Better it is to be of a humble spirit with the
meek and poor than to divide the spoil with
the proud.

—PROVERBS 16:19

Pride lands me flat on my face, but humility
prepares me for honor.

—PROVERBS 29:23 (THE MESSAGE)

The Lord has showed me what is good. And
what does the Lord require of me? To act
justly and to love mercy and to walk humbly
with my God.

—MICAH 6:8 (NLT)

I humble myself [feeling very insignificant] in
the presence of the Lord, and He will exalt me

[He will lift me up and make my life
significant].

—JAMES 4:10

I humble myself under the mighty hand of
God, and in his good time he will lift me up.

—1 PETER 5:6 (TLB)

☀ Insecurity ☀

THE LORD is my Light and my Salvation—
whom shall I fear or dread? The Lord is the
Refuge and Stronghold of my life—of whom
shall I be afraid?

—PSALM 27:1

I dwell in the secret place of the Most High
and abide under the shadow of the
Almighty. . . . He shall cover me with His
feathers, and under His wings I shall take
refuge; His truth shall be my shield and
buckler.

—PSALM 91:1, 4 (NKJV)

I hearken unto wisdom and I dwell securely
and in confident trust and I am quiet, without
fear or dread of evil.

—PROVERBS 1:33

In the reverent and worshipful fear of the
Lord I have strong confidence, and as His
child, I shall always have a place of refuge.

—PROVERBS 14:26

The name of the Lord is my strong tower;
the righteous run to it and are safe.

—PROVERBS 18:10 (NKJV)

I fear not, for God is with me; I am not dismayed; for He is my God. He will strengthen
me, yes, He will help me, He will uphold me
with His righteous right hand.

—ISAIAH 41:10 (NKJV)

No weapon formed against me shall prosper,
and every tongue that rises against me in
judgment I shall show to be in the wrong.
This [peace, righteousness, security, triumph
over opposition] is my inheritance because I
am a servant of the Lord.

—ISAIAH 54:17

I am assured and know that [God being a partner in my labor] all things work together and are [fitting into a plan] for good to and for me because I love God and I'm called according to [His] design and purpose.

—ROMANS 8:28

I am more than a conqueror and gain a surpassing victory through Him Who loved me. For I am persuaded beyond doubt (am sure) that neither death nor life, nor angels nor principalities, nor things impending and threatening nor things to come, nor powers, nor height nor depth, nor anything else in all creation will be able to separate me from the love of God which is in Christ Jesus my Lord. God loves me!

—ROMANS 8:37-39

God's grace is sufficient for me, for His strength is made perfect in weakness.

—2 CORINTHIANS 12:9 (NKJV)

I can do everything God asks me to with the help of Christ who gives me the strength and power.

—PHILIPPIANS 4:13 (TLB)

I can say without any doubt or fear, "The Lord is my Helper, and I am not afraid of anything that mere man can do to me."

—HEBREWS 13:6 (TLB)

⚜ Integrity ⚜

I am a person of my word. I swear to my own
hurt and do not change.

—PSALM 15:4

Integrity and uprightness preserve me, for I
wait for and expect the Lord.

—PSALM 25:21

I walk in my integrity; I [expectantly] trust in,
lean on, and rely on the Lord without
wavering and I shall not slide. I invite God to
examine me and prove me; test my heart and
my mind. For [His] loving-kindness is before
my eyes, and I walk in His truth [faithfully]. I
do not sit with false persons, nor fellowship
with pretenders; I hate the company of
evildoers and will not sit with the wicked.

—PSALM 26:1-5

When swelling and pride come, then emptiness and shame come also, but with the humble (those who are lowly, who have been pruned or chiseled by trial, and renounce self) are skillful and godly Wisdom and soundness. The integrity of the upright is my guide.

—PROVERBS 11:2-3

If anyone forces me to go one mile, I will go with him two [miles]. I choose the more excellent way even when no one is looking.

—MATTHEW 5:41

I live before God in all good conscience!

—ACTS 23:1 (TLB)

I always exercise and discipline myself [mortifying my body, deadening my carnal affections, bodily appetites, and worldly desires, endeavoring in all respects] to have a clear (unshaken, blameless) conscience, void of offense toward God and toward men.

—ACTS 24:16

I speak the truth in Christ. I do not lie; my conscience [enlightened and prompted] by the Holy Spirit bearing witness with me.

—ROMANS 9:1

I earnestly desire and zealously cultivate the greatest and best gifts and graces (the higher gifts and the choicest graces), and the more excellent way [one that is better by far and the highest of them all—love].

—1 CORINTHIANS 12:31

I have learned to sense what is vital, and approve and prize what is excellent and of real value [recognizing the highest and the best, and distinguishing the moral differences], that I may be untainted and pure and

unerring and blameless [so that with a heart
sincere and certain and unsullied, I may
approach] the day of Christ [not stumbling
nor causing others to stumble]. I abound in
and am filled with the fruits of righteousness
(of right standing with God and right doing)
which come through Jesus Christ (the
Anointed One), to the honor and praise of
God [that His glory may be both manifested
and recognized].

—PHILIPPIANS 1:10-11

The object and purpose of my instruction and
charge is love, which springs from a pure
heart and a good (clear) conscience and
sincere (unfeigned) faith.

—1 TIMOTHY 1:5

I hold fast to faith (that leaning of the entire
human personality on God in absolute trust
and confidence) and I have a good (clear)

conscience. By rejecting and thrusting from them [their conscience], some individuals have made shipwreck of their faith.

—1 TIMOTHY 1:19

The Lord's divine power has bestowed upon me all things that [are requisite and suited] to life and godliness, through the [full, personal] knowledge of Him Who called me by and to His own glory and excellence (virtue).

—2 PETER 1:3

❧ Laziness and Passivity ❧

I will not die for lack of discipline and
instruction, and in the greatness of my folly
be led astray and lost.

—PROVERBS 5:23

I give no [unnecessary] sleep to my eyes, nor
slumber to my eyelids. . . . Yet a little sleep, a
little slumber, a little folding of the hands to
lie down and sleep—so will poverty come
like a robber or one who travels [with slowly
but surely approaching steps] and my want
like an armed man [making me helpless].

—PROVERBS 6:4, 10-11

Better is he who is lightly esteemed but
works for his own support than he who
assumes honor for himself and lacks bread.

—PROVERBS 12:9

The sluggard does not plow when winter sets in; therefore he begs in harvest and has nothing.

—PROVERBS 20:4

The slothful and self-indulgent buries his hand in his bosom; it distresses and wearies him to bring it again to his mouth. I am neither slothful nor self-indulgent. I am not a sluggard who is wiser in his own eyes and conceit than seven men who can render a reason and answer discreetly.

—PROVERBS 26:15-16

Through idleness of the hands the house leaks.

—ECCLESIASTES 10:18

I have been raised with Christ [to a new life, thus sharing His resurrection from the dead]. I aim at and seek the [rich, eternal treasures] that are above, where Christ is, seated at the right hand of God.

—COLOSSIANS 3:1

I [strongly and earnestly] desire to show the same diligence and sincerity [all the way through] in realizing and enjoying the full assurance and development of [my] hope until the end, in order that I may not grow disinterested and become a [spiritual] sluggard, but an imitator, behaving as do those who through faith (by their leaning of the entire personality on God in Christ in absolute trust and confidence in His power, wisdom, and goodness) and by practice of patient endurance and waiting are [now] inheriting the promises.

—HEBREWS 6:11-12

Without faith it is impossible to please and be satisfactory to God. For to come near to God I

must [necessarily] believe that God exists and
that He is the rewarder of those who
earnestly and diligently seek Him [out].

—HEBREWS 11:6

God knows my [record of] works and what I
am doing. He would rather I were either cold
or hot—not lukewarm. For the lukewarm, He
will spew out of His mouth!

—REVELATION 3:15-16

✣ Loneliness ✣

God is with me and will keep (watch over me with care, take notice of) me wherever I may go.

—GENESIS 28:15

The Lord will not forsake me for His great name's sake, for it has pleased Him to make me one of His people.

—1 SAMUEL 12:22

[Lord] turn to me and be gracious to me, for I am lonely and afflicted.

—PSALM 25:16

If my father and mother should abandon me, the Lord would welcome and comfort me.

—PSALM 27:10 (TLB)

God is my refuge and strength, an ever-present help in trouble.

—PSALM 46:1 (NIV)

I do not fear, for God is with me; I am not dismayed, for He is my God. He will strengthen me and help me; He will uphold me with His righteous right hand.

—ISAIAH 41:10 (NIV)

The Lord is with me always, even unto the end of the world.

—MATTHEW 28:20 (KJV)

He will not abandon me or leave me as an orphan in the storm—He will come to me.

—JOHN 14:18 (TLB)

I will be a Father to you, and you shall be My sons and daughters, says the Lord Almighty.

—2 CORINTHIANS 6:18

My conduct will be without covetousness, and I will be content with such things as I have. For God Himself has said, "I will never leave you nor forsake you."

—HEBREWS 13:5 (NKJV)

✣ Patience ✣

I won't be impatient for the Lord to act! I will keep traveling steadily along his pathway and in due season He will honor me with every blessing.

—PSALM 37:34 (TLB)

I WAITED patiently and expectantly for the Lord; and He inclined to me and heard my cry.

—PSALM 40:1

Better is the end of a thing than the beginning of it, and the patient in spirit is better than the proud in spirit.

—ECCLESIASTES 7:8

[I will be full of joy now!] I will exult and triumph in my troubles and rejoice in my sufferings, knowing that pressure and affliction and hardship produce patient and

unswerving endurance. And endurance
(fortitude) develops maturity of character
(approved faith and tried integrity). And
character [of this sort] produces [the habit of]
joyful and confident hope of eternal salvation.

—ROMANS 5:3-4

I will not lose heart and grow weary and faint
in acting nobly and doing right, for in due
time and at the appointed season I will reap,
if I do not loosen and relax my courage and
faint.

—GALATIANS 6:9

I will be strengthened with all power
according to God's glorious might so that I
may have great endurance and patience, and
joyfully give thanks to the Father, Who has
qualified me to share in the inheritance of the
saints in the kingdom of light.

—COLOSSIANS 1:11-12 (NIV)

I do not want to become lazy, but I want to imitate those who through faith and patience inherit what has been promised.

—HEBREWS 6:12 (NIV)

I will be happy when the way is rough, because it gives my patience a chance to grow. So I will let it grow, and not try to squirm out of my problems. For when my patience is finally in full bloom, then I will be ready for anything, strong in character, full and complete.

—JAMES 1:2-4 (TLB)

I will be patient [as I wait] till the coming of the Lord, learning from the farmer who waits expectantly for the precious harvest from the land, keeping up his patient [vigil] over it until it receives the early and late rains. So I also will be patient. I will establish my heart [strengthen and confirm it in the final

certainty], for the coming of the Lord is very
near.

—JAMES 5:7-8

Because I have guarded and kept God's word
of patient endurance [have held fast the
lesson of His patience with the expectant
endurance that He gave me], He also will
keep me [safe] from the hour of trial (testing)
which is coming on the whole world to try
those who dwell upon the earth.

—REVELATION 3:10

✛ Peace ✛

I acquaint myself with Him [agree with God and show myself to be conformed to His will] and I am at peace; by that [I shall prosper and great] good shall come to me.

—JOB 22:21

I will listen to what God the Lord will say; He promises peace to His people, His saints. . . . Love and faithfulness meet together; righteousness and peace kiss each other. Faithfulness springs forth from the earth, and righteousness looks down from heaven.

—PSALM 85:8, 10-11 (NIV)

When I am trying to please God, He makes even my worst enemies to be at peace with me.

—PROVERBS 16:7 (TLB)

You will guard me and keep me in perfect
and constant peace as my mind [both its
inclination and its character] is stayed on You,
because I commit myself to You, lean on You,
and hope confidently in You.

—ISAIAH 26:3

The mountains shall depart, and the hills be
removed; but God's kindness shall not depart
from me, neither shall the covenant of His
peace be removed, saith the Lord that hath
mercy on me.

—ISAIAH 54:10 (KJV)

My righteousness (my rightness, my justice,
and my right relationship with God) shall go
before me [conducting me to peace and
prosperity], and the glory of the Lord shall be
my rear guard.

—ISAIAH 58:8

Peace I leave with you; My [own] peace I now give and bequeath to you. Not as the world gives do I give to you. Do not let your hearts be troubled, neither let them be afraid. [Stop allowing yourselves to be agitated and disturbed; and do not permit yourselves to be fearful and intimidated and cowardly and unsettled.]

—JOHN 14:27

God's peace [shall be mine, that tranquil state of a soul assured of its salvation through Christ, and so fearing nothing from God and being content with its earthly lot of whatever sort that is, that peace] which transcends all understanding shall garrison and mount guard over my heart and mind in Christ Jesus.

—PHILIPPIANS 4:7

Now may the Lord of peace Himself give me peace at all times and in every way.

—2 THESSALONIANS 3:16 (NIV)

I strive to live in peace with everybody and pursue that consecration and holiness without which no one will [ever] see the Lord.

—HEBREWS 12:14

⚜ Power ⚜

He gives power to the faint and weary, and to him who has no might He increases strength [causing it to multiply and making it to abound].

—ISAIAH 40:29

I have been given authority and power over all the power that the enemy [possesses]; and nothing shall in any way harm me.

—LUKE 10:19

I shall receive power (ability, efficiency, and might) when the Holy Spirit has come upon me, and I shall be His witness to the ends (the very bounds) of the earth.

—ACTS 1:8

Thanks be to God, Who gives me the victory [making me a conqueror] through my Lord Jesus Christ.

—1 CORINTHIANS 15:57

It is God Who confirms and makes me steadfast and establishes me and has consecrated and anointed me [enduing me with the gifts of the Holy Spirit]; [He has also appropriated and acknowledged me as His by] putting His seal upon me and giving me His [Holy] Spirit in my heart as the security deposit and guarantee [of the fulfillment of His promise].

—2 CORINTHIANS 1:21-22

The Lord says to me, My grace (My favor and loving-kindness and mercy) is enough for you [sufficient against any danger and enables you to bear the trouble manfully]; for My strength and power are made perfect (fulfilled and completed) and show themselves most effective in [your] weakness. Therefore, I will all the more gladly glory in my weaknesses and infirmities, that the strength and power

of Christ (the Messiah) may rest (yes, may
pitch a tent over and dwell) upon me!

—2 CORINTHIANS 12:9

God has granted me a spirit of wisdom and
revelation [of insight into mysteries and
secrets] in the [deep and intimate] knowledge
of Him . . . [so that I can know and under-
stand] what is the immeasurable and
unlimited and surpassing greatness of His
power in and for me and all who believe, as
demonstrated in the working of His mighty
strength.

—EPHESIANS 1:17, 19

May God grant me out of the rich treasury of
His glory to be strengthened and reinforced
with mighty power in the inner man by the
[Holy] Spirit [Himself indwelling my
innermost being and personality].

—EPHESIANS 3:16

God did not give me a spirit of timidity (of cowardice, of craven and cringing and fawning fear), but [He has given me a spirit] of power and of love and of calm and well-balanced mind and discipline and self-control.

—2 TIMOTHY 1:7

❖ Prayer ❖

I will pray to Him, and He will hear me, and I will fulfill my vows.

—JOB 22:27 (NIV)

I sought the Lord, and He heard me, and delivered me from all my fears. . . . The eyes of the Lord are on the righteous, and His ears are open to their cry.

—PSALM 34:4, 15 (NKJV)

In You, O Lord, do I hope; You will answer, O Lord my God.

—PSALM 38:15

The Lord is near to me and all who call upon Him, to all who call upon Him sincerely and in truth. He will fulfill the desires of those who reverently and worshipfully fear Him; He also will hear their cry and will save them.

—PSALM 145:18-19

The Lord is far from the wicked, but He hears my prayer—the prayer of the [consistently] righteous (the upright, in right standing with Him).

—PROVERBS 15:29

I seek, inquire for, and require the Lord while He may be found [claiming Him by necessity and by right]; I call upon Him while He is near.

—ISAIAH 55:6

I ask and keep on asking and I receive. I seek and keep on seeking and I find. I knock and keep on knocking and the door is opened unto me.

—MATTHEW 7:7-8

Again I tell you, if two of you on earth agree (harmonize together, make a symphony together) about whatever [anything and everything] they may ask, it will come to pass and be done for them by My Father in heaven.

—MATTHEW 18:19

I always pray, I don't faint, quit or give up.

—LUKE 18:1

I ask and receive and my joy is made full.

—JOHN 16:24 (NKJV)

The [Holy] Spirit comes to my aid and bears me up in my weakness; for I do not know what prayer to offer nor how to offer it worthily as I ought, but the Spirit Himself goes to meet my supplication and pleads in my behalf with unspeakable yearnings and groanings too deep for utterance.

—ROMANS 8:26

I will be unceasing in prayer [praying perseveringly].

—1 THESSALONIANS 5:17

I will fearlessly and confidently and boldly draw near to the throne of grace (the throne of God's unmerited favor to sinners), that I may receive mercy [for my failures] and find grace to help in good time for every need [appropriate help and well-timed help, coming just when I need it].

—HEBREWS 4:16

✣ Prosperity, Finances, and Giving ✣

I remember the Lord my God, for it is He who gives me the ability to produce wealth, and so confirms His covenant, which He swore to my forefathers.

—DEUTERONOMY 8:18 (NIV)

The Lord shall command the blessing upon me in my storehouse and in all that I undertake. . . . The Lord makes me to have a surplus of prosperity through the fruit of my body. He blesses me in the land which He gives me.

—DEUTERONOMY 28:8, 11

I am like a tree firmly planted by the streams of water, ready to bring forth its fruit in its season; its leaf also shall not fade or wither;

and everything I do shall prosper [and come to maturity].

—PSALM 1:3

Because I seek (inquire of and require) the Lord [by right of my need and on the authority of His Word], I shall not lack any beneficial thing.

—PSALM 34:10

When I bring all the tithes (the whole tenth of my income) into the storehouse, that there may be food in God's house, the Lord of hosts will open the windows of heaven for me and pour me out such a blessing that there won't be room enough to receive it.

—MALACHI 3:10

When I give to the needy, I do not let my left hand know what my right hand is doing, so that my giving may be in secret. Then my

Father, who sees what is done in secret, will reward me.

—MATTHEW 6:3-4 (NIV)

I do not store up for myself treasures on earth, where moth and rust destroy, and where thieves break in and steal. But I store up for myself treasures in heaven, where moth and rust do not destroy, and where thieves do not break in and steal. For where my treasure is, there my heart will be also.

—MATTHEW 6:19-21 (NIV)

I give, and [gifts] are given to me; good measure, pressed down, shaken together, and running over. For with the measure I deal out [with the measure I use when I confer benefits on others], it will be measured back to me.

—LUKE 6:38

My prayers and gifts to the poor have come up as a memorial offering before God.

—ACTS 10:5 (NIV)

I keep out of debt and owe no man anything, except to love others.

—ROMANS 13:8

If I sow sparingly and grudgingly, I will also reap sparingly and grudgingly, and if I sow generously [that blessings may come to someone] I will also reap generously and with blessings. I [give] as I have made up my own mind and purposed in my heart, not reluctantly or sorrowfully or under compulsion, for God loves (He takes pleasure in, prizes above other things, and is unwilling to abandon or to do without) a cheerful (joyous, "prompt to do it") giver [whose heart is in his giving].

—2 CORINTHIANS 9:6-7

My God will meet all my needs according to His glorious riches in Christ Jesus.

—PHILIPPIANS 4:19 (NIV)

God wants me to prosper and be in health, even as my soul prospers.

—3 JOHN 2 (KJV)

❧ Protection ❧

The eternal God is my refuge and dwelling place, and underneath are the everlasting arms.
—DEUTERONOMY 33:27

I am secure and feel confident because there is hope; yes, I look around me and take my rest in safety. I lie down, and none make me afraid.

—JOB 11:18-19

The Lord is my refuge and high tower when I am oppressed, a refuge and stronghold in my time of trouble.

—PSALM 9:9

You are my hiding place from every storm of life; you even keep me from getting into trouble! You surround me with songs of victory.

—PSALM 32:7 (TLB)

I trust in and confidently rely on the loving-kindness and the mercy of God forever and ever. I will thank You and confide in You forever, because You have done it [delivered me and kept me safe]. I will wait on, hope in and expect in Your name.

—PSALM 52:8-9

As I dwell in the secret place of the Most High, I shall abide under the shadow of the Almighty. I will say of the Lord, "He is my refuge and my fortress; My God, in Him I will trust."

—PSALM 91:1-2 (NKJV)

Because God is my refuge, the High God my very own home, evil can't get close to me, harm can't get through the door. He ordered his angels to guard me wherever I go.

—PSALM 91:9-11 (THE MESSAGE)

In the reverent and worshipful fear of the Lord I have strong confidence, and I shall always have a place of refuge.

—PROVERBS 14:26

By two unchangeable things [His promise and His oath] in which it is impossible for God ever to prove false or deceive me, I, who have fled [to Him] for refuge have mighty indwelling strength and strong encouragement to grasp and hold fast the hope appointed for me and set before [me].

—HEBREWS 6:18

⚜ Receiving God's Love ⚜

God loves those who love Him, and those who seek Him early and diligently shall find Him.

—PROVERBS 8:17

For God so greatly loved and dearly prized the world that He [even] gave up His only begotten (unique) Son, so that whoever believes in (trusts in, clings to, relies on) Him shall not perish (come to destruction, be lost) but have eternal (everlasting) life.

—JOHN 3:16

He has loved me, [just] as the Father has loved Him; and He instructs me to abide in His love [to continue in the Father's love with Him].

—JOHN 15:9

For the Father Himself [tenderly] loves me
because I have loved Him and have believed
that He came out from the Father.

—JOHN 16:27

Hope never disappoints or deludes or shames
me, for God's love has been poured out in my
heart through the Holy Spirit Who has been
given to me.

—ROMANS 5:5

I love God truly [with affectionate reverence,
prompt obedience, and grateful recognition of
His blessing], I am known by God [recog-
nized as worthy of His intimacy and love,
and I am owned by Him].

—1 CORINTHIANS 8:3

Let everything I do be done in love (true love
to God and man as inspired by God's love
for me).

—1 CORINTHIANS 16:14

The love of Christ controls and urges and impels me, because I am of the opinion and conviction that [if] One died for all, then all died; and He died for all, so that all those who live might live no longer to and for themselves, but to and for Him Who died and was raised again for our sake.

—2 CORINTHIANS 5:14-15

Christ through my faith [actually] dwells (settles down, abides, makes His permanent home) in my heart! I am rooted deep in love and founded securely on love, I have the power and strength to apprehend and grasp with all the saints [God's devoted people, the experience of that love] what is the breadth and length and height and depth [of it]; [I have come] to know [practically, through experience for myself] the love of Christ, which far surpasses mere knowledge [without experience]; I am filled [through all my being] unto all the fullness of God [I have the richest measure of the divine Presence, and I have become a body wholly filled and flooded with God Himself]!

—EPHESIANS 3:17-19

My life lovingly expresses truth [in all things, speaking truly, dealing truly, living truly]. Enfolded in love, I grow up in every way and in all things into Him Who is the Head, [even] Christ (the Messiah, the Anointed One).

—EPHESIANS 4:15

I walk in love, [esteeming and delighting in others] as Christ loved me and gave Himself up for me, a slain offering and sacrifice to God [for me, so that it became] a sweet fragrance.

—EPHESIANS 5:2

I know (understand, recognize, am conscious of, by observation and by experience) and believe (adhere to and put faith in and rely on) the love God cherishes for me. God is love, and I and all who dwell and continue in love dwell and continue in God, and God dwells and continues in us.

—1 JOHN 4:16

My love for Him comes as a result of His loving me first.

—1 JOHN 4:19 (TLB)

I carefully build myself up in this most holy faith by praying in the Holy Spirit, staying right at the center of God's love, keeping my arms open and outstretched, ready for the mercy of my Master, Jesus Christ. This is the unending life, the real life!

—JUDE 20-21 (THE MESSAGE)

⸰⸱ Rejection ⸰⸱

I will set My dwelling in and among you, and My soul shall not despise or reject or separate itself from you.

—LEVITICUS 26:11

If God be for me, who can be against me?

—ROMANS 8:31 (KJV)

Amid all these things I am more than a conqueror and gain a surpassing victory through Him Who loved me.

—ROMANS 8:37

No weapon that is formed against me shall prosper, and every tongue that shall rise against me in judgment I shall show to be in the wrong. This [peace, righteousness, security, triumph over opposition] is the heritage of the servants of the Lord.

—ISAIAH 54:17

Long before God laid down earth's foundations, He had me in mind, had settled on me as the focus of His love, to be made whole and holy by His love. Long, long ago He decided to adopt me into His family through Jesus Christ. (What pleasure He took in planning this!) He wanted me to enter into the celebration of His lavish gift-giving by the hand of His beloved Son.

—EPHESIANS 1:4-6 (THE MESSAGE)

God has chosen me.

—JOHN 15:16

I will be strong, vigorous, and very courageous. I will not be afraid, neither will I be dismayed, for the Lord my God is with me wherever I go. He never rejects me but has promised to be with me always.

—JOSHUA 1:9 & MATTHEW 28:20

When I go someplace and the people don't receive and accept me, I don't let it get me down, I just shake it off and go on about my business.

—LUKE 10:10-11

⸭ Seeking God ⸭

I will find the Lord when I seek Him with all
my heart and with all my soul.

—DEUTERONOMY 4:29 (NKJV)

I am called by Your name. I humble myself,
pray, seek, crave, and require of necessity
Your face and turn from my wicked ways. In
doing this, You have promised to hear from
heaven, forgive my sin, and heal my land.

—2 CHRONICLES 7:14

I seek You [inquiring for and of You, craving
You as my soul's first necessity], and I am
found by you.

—2 CHRONICLES 15:2

One thing I ask of the Lord, this is what I
seek: that I may dwell in the house of the
Lord all the days of my life, to gaze upon the

beauty of the Lord and to seek him in his temple.

—PSALM 27:4 (NIV)

The Lord is good to those who wait hopefully and expectantly for Him, to those who seek Him [inquire of and for Him and require Him by right of necessity and on the authority of God's word]. He does not willingly and from His heart afflict or grieve the children of men.

—LAMENTATIONS 3:25, 33

I seek (aim at and strive after) first of all His kingdom and His righteousness (His way of doing and being right), and then all these things taken together will be given me besides.

—MATTHEW 6:33

When I ask, it will be given to me; when I seek, I will find; when I knock, it will be opened to me. For everyone who aks receives, and he who seeks finds, and to him who knocks it will be opened.

—MATTHEW 7:7, 8 (NKJV)

I do not seek [by meditating and reasoning to inquire into] what I am to eat and what I am to drink; nor is my mind anxious [troubled, unsettled, excited, worried, and in suspense]. I only aim at and strive for and seek His kingdom, and all these things shall be supplied to me also.

—LUKE 12:29, 31

By myself I can do nothing; I judge only as I hear, and my judgment is just, for I seek not to please myself but him who sent me.

—JOHN 5:30 (NIV)

I have been raised with Christ [to a new life, thus sharing His resurrection from the dead]. I aim at and seek the [rich, eternal treasures] that are above, where Christ is, seated at the right hand of God.

—COLOSSIANS 3:1

Without faith it is impossible to please and be satisfactory to God. For to come near to God I must [necessarily] believe that God exists and that He is the rewarder of those who earnestly and diligently seek Him [out].

—HEBREWS 11:6

✢ Self-Control ✢

I will not be hot-tempered, stirring up dissension, but I will be patient, calming a quarrel.

—PROVERBS 15:18 (NIV)

I operate in self-control and don't allow my spirit to be unruly. I refuse to be like a city that is broken down and without walls. Self-control and discipline add protection to my life.

—PROVERBS 25:28

I seriously consider what I am doing before taking on new projects. I expand prudently and I do not court neglect of present duties by assuming too many new ones.

—PROVERBS 31:16

I am not rash with my mouth, and my heart is not hasty to utter words before God.

—ECCLESIASTES 5:2

When I vow a vow, I do not put off paying it.
I keep my promises.

—ECCLESIASTES 5:4

I will not be quick in spirit to be angry or
vexed, for anger and vexation lodge in the
bosom of fools.

—ECCLESIASTES 7:9

It is good that I should hope in and wait
quietly for the salvation (the safety and ease)
of the Lord. It is good that I should bear the
yoke [of divine disciplinary dealings].

—LAMENTATIONS 3:26-27

By my steadfastness and patient endurance I
shall win the true life of my soul.

—LUKE 21:19

Everything is permissible (allowable and
lawful) for me; but not all things are helpful
(good for me to do, expedient and profitable

when considered with other things). Everything is lawful for me, but I will not become the slave of anything or be brought under its power.

—1 CORINTHIANS 6:12

I walk in love. Love endures long and is patient and kind; love never is envious nor boils over with jealousy, is not boastful or vainglorious, does not display itself haughtily. It is not conceited (arrogant and inflated with pride); it is not rude (unmannerly) and does not act unbecomingly. Love (God's love in me) does not insist on its own rights or its own way, for it is not self-seeking; it is not touchy or fretful or resentful; it takes no account of the evil done to it [it pays no attention to a suffered wrong].

—1 CORINTHIANS 13:4-5

The fruit of the [Holy] Spirit [the work which His presence within accomplishes] is love, joy (gladness), peace, patience (an even temper, forbearance), kindness, goodness (benevolence), faithfulness, gentleness (meekness, humility), self-control (self-restraint, continence). Against such things there is no law [that can bring a charge].

—GALATIANS 5:22-23

Chosen by God for this new life of love, I dress in the wardrobe He picked out for me: compassion, kindness, humility, quiet strength, discipline. I am even-tempered, content with second place, quick to forgive an offense. I forgive as quickly and completely as the Master forgave me. And regardless of what else I put on, I wear love. It is my basic, all-purpose garment. I never want to be without it.

—COLOSSIANS 3:12-14 (THE MESSAGE)

I add my diligence [to the divine promises],
employing every effort in exercising my faith
to develop virtue, knowledge, self-control,
steadfastness, godliness, brotherly affection
and Christian love.

—2 PETER 1:5-7

✢ Selfishness ✢

I am blessed and I am a blessing to people.
I dispense good to others.

—GENESIS 12:2

If I give to the poor I will not want, but if I
hide my eyes [from their want] I will have
many a curse.

—PROVERBS 28:27

I am not selfish and self-centered, I deny
myself, I take up my cross and follow Jesus.
I forget myself, lose sight of myself and all
my own interests.

—MARK 8:34

I will love others with brotherly affection [as
members of one family], giving precedence
and showing honor to them.

—ROMANS 12:10

I make it a practice to please (make happy)
my neighbor for his good and for his true
welfare, to edify him [to strengthen him and
build him up spiritually].

—ROMANS 15:2

Although I am free in every way from
anyone's control, I have made myself a bond
servant to everyone, so that I might gain the
more [for Christ].

—1 CORINTHIANS 9:19

I must not think only of myself but try to
think of the other fellow, too, and what is
best for him.

—1 CORINTHIANS 10:24 (TLB)

I strive to please [to accommodate myself to
the opinions, desires, and interests of others,
adapting myself to] all men in everything I
do, not aiming at or considering my own

profit and advantage, but that of the many in order that they may be saved.

—1 CORINTHIANS 10:33

Christ died for all, so that all those who live might live no longer to and for themselves, but to and for Him Who died and was raised again for their sake.

—2 CORINTHIANS 5:15

I will bear (endure, carry) the burdens and troublesome moral faults of others, and in this way fulfill and observe perfectly the law of Christ (the Messiah) and complete what is lacking [in my obedience to it].

—GALATIANS 6:2

I do nothing out of selfish ambition or vain conceit, but in humility consider others better than myself. I look not only to my own interests, but also to the interests of others. My attitude is the same as that of Christ

Jesus: Who, being in very nature God, did not consider equality with God something to be grasped, but made himself nothing.

—PHILIPPIANS 2:3-7 (NIV)

I don't live just for pleasure and self-gratification [giving myself up to luxury and self-indulgence] for the one who does is dead even while they still live.

—1 TIMOTHY 5:6

But whoever has this world's goods, and sees his brother in need, and shuts up his heart from him, how does the love of God abide in him? I do not love in word or in tongue, but in deed and in truth.

—1 JOHN 3:17-18 (NKJV)

⚜ Spiritual Warfare ⚜

The Lord causes my enemies who rise up
against me to be defeated before my face;
they shall come out against me one way and
flee before me seven ways.

—DEUTERONOMY 28:7

The Lord contends with those who contend
with me; He fights against those who fight
against me! I take hold of the shield and
buckler, and stand up for my help! I draw out
also the spear and javelin and close up the
way of those who pursue and persecute me.
The Lord is my deliverance!

—PSALM 35:1-3

I discern in my bodily members [in the
sensitive appetites and wills of the flesh] a
different law (rule of action) at war against
the law of my mind (my reason) and making
me a prisoner to the law of sin that dwells in

my bodily organs [in the sensitive appetites and wills of the flesh]. Who will release and deliver me from [the shackles of] this body of death? O thank God! [He will!] through Jesus Christ (the Anointed One) my Lord!

—ROMANS 7:23-25

I am more than a conqueror through Christ Who loves me.

—ROMANS 8:37

Though I walk (live) in the flesh, I am not carrying on my warfare according to the flesh and using mere human weapons. For the weapons of my warfare are not physical [weapons of flesh and blood], but they are mighty before God for the overthrow and destruction of strongholds.

—2 CORINTHIANS 10:3-4

I will put on God's whole armor [the armor of a heavy-armed soldier which God supplies], that I may be able successfully to stand up

against [all] the strategies and the deceits of
the devil.

—EPHESIANS 6:11

I will fight on for God, holding tightly to the
eternal life which God has given me, and
which I have confessed with such a ringing
confession before many witnesses.

—1 TIMOTHY 6:12 (TLB)

I abstain from the sensual urges (the evil
desires, the passions of the flesh, my lower
nature) that wage war against my soul. I must
conduct myself properly (honorably,
righteously).

—1 PETER 2:11-12

I will be well balanced (temperate, sober of
mind), vigilant and cautious at all times; for
that enemy of mine, the devil, roams around
like a lion roaring [in fierce hunger], seeking
someone to seize upon and devour.

—1 PETER 5:8

❧ Stress ❧

I will commit my way to the Lord [roll and repose each care of my load on Him]; I will trust (lean on, rely on, and be confident) also in Him and He will bring it to pass.

—PSALM 37:5

It is useless to be in turmoil; heaping up riches, not knowing who will gather them.

—PSALM 39:6

It is vain for me to rise up early, to take rest late, to eat the bread of [anxious] toil—for He gives [blessings] to His beloved in sleep.

—PSALM 127:2

He gives power to the faint and weary, and to him who has no might He increases strength [causing it to multiply and making it to abound].

—ISAIAH 40:29

I will stop being perpetually uneasy (anxious and worried) about my life, what I shall eat or what I shall drink; or about my body, what I shall put on. Is not life greater [in quality] than food, and the body [far above and more excellent] than clothing? . . . I will not worry and be anxious . . . but I will seek (aim at and strive after) first of all the kingdom of God and His righteousness (His way of doing and being right), and then all these things taken together will be given to me besides.

—MATTHEW 6:25, 31, 33

I will guard against the cares and anxieties of the world and distractions of the age, and the pleasure and delight and false glamour and deceitfulness of riches, and the craving and passionate desire for other things that creep in and choke and suffocate the Word, causing it to become fruitless.

—MARK 4:19

Consider the lilies, how they grow. They
neither [wearily] toil nor spin nor weave; yet
I tell you, even Solomon in all his glory (his
splendor and magnificence) was not arrayed
like one of these.

—LUKE 12:27

I will take heed and be on guard, lest my
heart be overburdened and depressed
(weighed down) with the giddiness and
headache and nausea of self-indulgence,
drunkenness, and worldly worries and cares
pertaining to [the business of] this life, and
[lest] that day come upon me suddenly like a
trap or a noose.

—LUKE 21:34

It is God's desire that I be free from all
anxiety and distressing care.

—1 CORINTHIANS 7:32

I cannot do everything so I choose those things which are vital and excellent and of real value. I have wisdom and I am able to distinguish the highest and the best things for me to do.

—PHILIPPIANS 1:10

I will not fret or have any anxiety about anything, but in every circumstance and in everything, by prayer and petition (definite requests), with thanksgiving, continue to make my wants known to God.

—PHILIPPIANS 4:6

I do my best to fill my mind and meditate on things that are true, noble, reputable, authentic, compelling, gracious—the best, not the worst; the beautiful, not the ugly; things to praise, not things to curse. I put into practice what I've learned, what I've heard and seen and realized. As I do that, God, who makes everything work together, will work me into his most excellent harmonies.

—PHILIPPIANS 4:8-9 (THE MESSAGE)

I cast the whole of my care [all my anxieties, all my worries, all my concerns, once and for all] on Him, for He cares for me affectionately and cares about me watchfully.

—1 PETER 5:7

❧ Submission to Authority ❧
God's and Man's

The Lord my God I will serve; His voice I will obey.

—JOSHUA 24:24

Rebellion is as the sin of witchcraft and stubbornness is idolatry, therefore I am submissive to authority.

—1 SAMUEL 15:23

The mercy and loving-kindness of the Lord are from everlasting to everlasting upon me and all who reverently and worshipfully fear Him. To such as keep His covenant [hearing, receiving, loving, and obeying it] and to those who [earnestly] remember His commandments to do them [imprinting them on their hearts].

—PSALM 103:17-18

I am blessed (happy, fortunate, to be envied) because I fear (revere and worship) the Lord. I delight greatly in His commandments.

—PSALM 112:1

I will keep [God's] law continually, forever and ever [hearing, receiving, loving, and obeying it]. And I will walk at liberty and at ease, for I have sought and inquired for [and desperately required] His precepts.

—PSALM 119:44-45

If I am willing and obedient, I will eat the good of the land; but if I refuse and rebel, I will be devoured by the sword. For the mouth of the Lord has spoken it.

—ISAIAH 1:19-20

Blessed (happy and to be envied) am I because I hear the Word of God and obey and practice it!

—LUKE 11:28

As an employee I am obedient to my boss and have respect for him or her. I am eager to please them in singleness of motive and with all my heart, as a service to Christ Himself.

—EPHESIANS 6:5

I submit to God, I resist the devil and he flees from me. I draw near to God and He draws near to me.

—JAMES 4:7-8 (NKJV)

As an employee I am submissive to my employer. I show him or her respect, not only when they are good and kind to me but at all times for God approves of me when I do so.

—1 PETER 2:18-19

I receive from God whatever I ask, because I [watchfully] obey His orders [observe His suggestions and injunctions, follow His plan for me] and [habitually] practice what is pleasing to Him.

—1 JOHN 3:22

For Wives

Because I [really] love the Lord, I will keep (obey) His commands.

—JOHN 14:15

I am loyally subject to the governing (civil) authorities, for there is no authority except from God [by His permission, His sanction], and those who exist do so by God's appointment.

—ROMANS 13:1

I don't resist authority because if I did I would be resisting what God has appointed and arranged [in divine order]. I would bring down judgment on myself and receive the penalty due. I am submissive to authority.

—ROMANS 13:2

I love God truly [with affectionate reverence, prompt obedience, and grateful recognition of

His blessing], and I am known by God [recognized as worthy of His intimacy and love, and I am owned by Him].

—1 CORINTHIANS 8:3

I am submissive to my husband and adapt myself to him. I conduct myself with purity and modesty. I reverence my husband and that includes respect, honor, esteem, and appreciation. I prize him highly, I admire him, I am devoted to him, I deeply love and enjoy my husband.

—1 PETER 3:1-2

⚜ Taking Care of Your Body ⚜

I will serve the Lord my God, and He will
bless my bread and my water and take
sickness away from me.

—EXODUS 23:25 (NKJV)

I will reverently fear and worship the Lord
and turn [entirely] away from evil. It shall be
health to my nerves and sinews, and marrow
and moistening to my bones.

—PROVERBS 3:7-8

I will hear and receive Your sayings, and the
years of my life will be many.

—PROVERBS 4:10 (NKJV)

I will attend to God's words; consent and
submit to His sayings. I will not let them
depart from my sight but will keep them in
the center of my heart. For they are life to

those who find them, healing and health to all their flesh.

—PROVERBS 4:20-22

Pleasant words are as a honeycomb, sweet to the mind and healing to the body.

—PROVERBS 16:24

A happy heart is good medicine and a cheerful mind works healing, but a broken spirit dries up the bones.

—PROVERBS 17:22

He who is loose and slack in his work is brother to him who is a destroyer and he who does not use his endeavors to heal himself is brother to him who commits suicide.

—PROVERBS 18:9

I will restore health to you, and I will heal
your wounds, says the Lord.

—JEREMIAH 30:17

I don't give food a place in my life that is out
of balance because God said, "Food [is
intended] for the stomach and the stomach
for food, but God will finally end [the func-
tions of] both and bring them to nothing."
I don't get involved in sexual immorality
because God said, "The body is not intended
for sexual immorality, but [is intended] for
the Lord, and the Lord [is intended] for the
body [to save, sanctify, and raise it again]."

—1 CORINTHIANS 6:13

My body is the temple (the very sanctuary)
of the Holy Spirit Who lives within me,
Whom I have received [as a Gift] from God.
I am not my own, I was bought with a price

[purchased with a preciousness and paid for, made His own].

—1 CORINTHIANS 6:19-20

The God of peace Himself sanctifies me through and through [separates me from profane things, makes me pure and wholly consecrated to God]; and my spirit and soul and body are preserved sound and complete [and will be found] blameless at the coming of our Lord Jesus Christ (the Messiah).

—1 THESSALONIANS 5:23

I will live a balanced life because God's Word states that if we are not well balanced we open a door for Satan to come in and devour us.

—1 PETER 5:8

I prosper in every way and [my body] keeps well, even as my soul keeps well and prospers.

—3 JOHN 2

✤ Temptation ✤

God is my Refuge and Strength [mighty and impenetrable to temptation], a very present and well-proved help in trouble.

—PSALM 46:1

In the day when I called, You answered me; and You strengthened me with strength (might and inflexibility to temptation) in my inner self.

—PSALM 138:3

Teach me to do Your will, for You are my God; let Your good Spirit lead me into a level country and into the land of uprightness.

—PSALM 143:10

If sinners entice me, I will not consent. . . . I will not walk in the way with them.

—PROVERBS 1:10, 15

I will enter not into the path of the wicked, and go not in the way of evil men. I will avoid it, turn from it and pass on.

—PROVERBS 4:14-15

I keep awake and watch and pray [constantly], that I may not enter into temptation; the spirit indeed is willing, but the flesh is weak.

—MARK 14:38

I pray to God that I will not be overcome by temptation.

—LUKE 22:40 (TLB)

I will not let myself be overcome with evil, but will overcome (master) evil with good.

—ROMANS 12:21

Blessed (happy, to be envied) am I when I'm patient under trial and stand up under temptation, for when I have stood the test and been approved, I will receive [the victor's] crown of life which God has promised to those who love Him.

—JAMES 1:12

I will be subject to God. I will resist the devil [stand firm against him], and he will flee from me.

—JAMES 4:7

❧ The Goodness of God ❧

O taste and see that the Lord [our God] is good! Blessed (happy, fortunate, to be envied) is the man who trusts and takes refuge in Him.

—PSALM 34:8

I seek my happiness in the Lord, and he gives me my heart's desire. I give myself to the Lord; trust in him, and he helps me; he makes my righteousness shine like the noonday sun.

—PSALM 37:4-6 (GNT)

The Lord God is my Sun and Shield; the Lord bestows [present] grace and favor and [future] glory (honor, splendor, and heavenly bliss)! No good thing will He withhold from me as I walk uprightly.

—PSALM 84:11

Praise the Lord! For the Lord is good; sing praises to His name, for He is gracious and lovely!

—PSALM 135:3

The Lord is good to everyone and His tender mercies are over all His works.

—PSALM 145:9

The blessing of the Lord—it makes me [truly] rich, and He adds no sorrow with it.

—PROVERBS 10:22

God has good thoughts and plans toward me. He intends for me to have peace and not evil and to give me hope in my final outcome.

—JEREMIAH 29:11

The Lord is good; for His mercy, tender kindness and steadfast love endure forever.

—JEREMIAH 33:11

The Lord is good, a Strength and Stronghold in my day of trouble; He knows (recognizes, has knowledge of, and understands) me because I take refuge and trust in Him.

—NAHUM 1:7

I will not be seized with alarm and struck with fear, for it is my Father's good pleasure to give me the kingdom!

—LUKE 12:32

The goodness of God leads men to repentance.

—ROMANS 2:4 (NKJV)

Eye has not seen and ear has not heard and has not entered into the heart of man, [all that] God has prepared (made and keeps ready) for me because I love Him [I hold Him in affectionate reverence, promptly obeying

Him and gratefully recognizing the benefits
He has bestowed].

—1 CORINTHIANS 2:9

My God will liberally supply (fill to the full)
my every need according to His riches in
glory in Christ Jesus.

—PHILIPPIANS 4:19

⭮ The Mind ⭯

O Lord, you have searched me [thoroughly]
and have known me. You know my down-
sitting and my uprising; You understand my
thought afar off. You sift and search out
my path and my lying down, and You are
acquainted with all my ways. For there is not
a word in my tongue [still unuttered], but,
behold, O Lord, You know it altogether.

—PSALM 139:1-4

I lean on, trust in, and am confident in the
Lord with all my heart and mind and do not
rely on my own insight or understanding. In
all my ways, I know, recognize, and
acknowledge Him, and He directs and makes
straight and plain my paths.

—PROVERBS 3:5-6

I think about sticking with things because the
thoughts of the diligent tend only to plenty,

but everyone who is impatient and hasty
hastens only to want.

—PROVERBS 21:5

As I think in my heart, so am I.

—PROVERBS 23:7

I will not be conformed to this world (this
age), [fashioned after and adapted to its
external, superficial customs], but be transformed (changed) by the [entire] renewal of
my mind [by its new ideals and its new
attitude], so that I may prove [for myself]
what is the good and acceptable and perfect
will of God, even the thing which is good and
acceptable and perfect [in His sight for me].

—ROMANS 12:2

I refute arguments and theories and reasonings and every proud and lofty thing that sets
itself up against the [true] knowledge of God;
and I lead every thought and purpose away

captive into the obedience of Christ (the
Messiah, the Anointed one).

—2 CORINTHIANS 10:5

I strip myself of my former nature [put off
and discard my old unrenewed self] which
characterized my previous manner of life. I
am constantly being renewed in the spirit of
my mind [having a fresh mental and spiritual
attitude], and I put on the new nature (the
regenerate self) created in God's image,
[Godlike] in true righteousness and holiness.

—EPHESIANS 4:22-24

Whatever is true, whatever is worthy of
reverence and is honorable and seemly,
whatever is just, whatever is pure, whatever
is lovely and lovable, whatever is kind and
winsome and gracious, if there is any virtue
and excellence, if there is anything worthy of
praise, I will think on and weigh and take

account of these things [fix my mind on them].

—PHILIPPIANS 4:8

God has not given me a spirit of fear, but of power, love, and a sound mind.

—2 TIMOTHY 1:7 (KJV)

ᛘ The Power of Words ᛘ

May the words of my mouth and the
meditation of my heart be pleasing in your
sight, O Lord, my Rock and my Redeemer.

—PSALM 19:14 (NIV)

Keep my tongue from evil and my lips from
speaking deceit.

—PSALM 34:13

Help me, Lord, to keep my mouth shut and
my lips sealed.

—PSALM 141:3 (TLB)

The mouth of the [uncompromisingly]
righteous man is a well of life, but the mouth
of the wicked conceals violence.

—PROVERBS 10:11

The mouths of the righteous (those
harmonious with God) bring forth skillful and

godly Wisdom, but the perverse tongue shall be cut down [like a barren and rotten tree].

—PROVERBS 10:31

He who guards his mouth keeps his life, but he who opens wide his lips comes to ruin.

—PROVERBS 13:3

A soft answer turns away wrath, but grievous words stir up anger.

—PROVERBS 15:1

I have joy in making an apt answer, and a word spoken at the right moment—how good it is!

—PROVERBS 15:23

I think before I speak because the mind of the wise instructs his mouth.

—PROVERBS 16:23

The power of life and death are in the tongue, and they who indulge in it shall eat the fruit of it [for death or life].

—PROVERBS 18:21

A word fitly spoken and in due season is like apples of gold in settings of silver.

—PROVERBS 25:11

The Master, God, has given me a well-taught tongue, so I know how to encourage tired people. He wakes me up in the morning, wakes me up, opens my ears to listen as one ready to take orders.

—ISAIAH 50:4 (THE MESSAGE)

Out of the fullness (the overflow, the superabundance) of the heart the mouth speaks. The good man from his inner good treasure flings forth good things, and the evil man out of his inner evil storehouse flings forth evil things.

—MATTHEW 12:34-35

On the day of judgment I will have to give account for every idle (inoperative, nonworking) word I speak. For by my words I will be justified and acquitted, and by my words I will be condemned and sentenced.

—MATTHEW 12:36-37

Let no foul or polluting language, nor evil word nor unwholesome or worthless talk [ever] come out of my mouth, but only such [speech] as is good and beneficial to the spiritual progress of others, as is fitting to the need and the occasion, that it may be a blessing and give grace (God's favor) to those who hear it.

—EPHESIANS 4:29

I want to enjoy life and see good days [good—whether apparent or not] so I keep my tongue free from evil and my lips from guile (treachery, deceit).

—1 PETER 3:10

⚜ Trust ⚜

As for God, His way is perfect; the word of the Lord is tried. He is a Shield to me because I trust and take refuge in Him. For who is God but the Lord? And who is a Rock except our God? God is my strong Fortress; He guides the blameless in His way and sets me free.

—2 SAMUEL 22:31-33

I am blessed (happy, fortunate, and to be envied) because I seek refuge and put my trust in the Lord.

—PSALM 2:12

The Lord is my Rock, my Fortress, and my Deliverer; my God, my keen and firm Strength in Whom I trust and take refuge, my Shield, and the Horn of my salvation, my High Tower. I call upon the Lord, Who is to be praised; so shall I be saved from my enemies.

—PSALM 18:2-3

Some trust in chariots, and some in horses; but I remember the name of the Lord my God.

—PSALM 20:7 (NKJV)

I trust in, rely on, and am confident in You, O Lord; I say, You are my God. My times are in Your hands.

—PSALM 31:14-15

When I am afraid, I will trust in You. In God, whose word I praise, in God I trust; I will not be afraid. What can mortal man do to me?

—PSALM 56:3-4 (NIV)

I trust in God at all times. I pour out my heart before Him; God is a refuge for me.

—PSALM 62:8

I lean on, trust in, and am confident in the
Lord with all my heart and mind and I do not
rely on my own insight or understanding. In
all my ways I know, recognize, and acknowledge Him, and He directs and makes straight
and plain my paths. I am not wise in my own
eyes; I reverently fear and worship the Lord
and turn [entirely] away from evil. It shall be
health to my nerves and sinews, and marrow
and moistening to my bones.

—PROVERBS 3:5-8

The fear of man brings a snare, but whoever
leans on, trusts in, and puts his confidence in
the Lord is safe and set on high.

—PROVERBS 29:25

In repentance and rest is my salvation, in
quietness and trust is my strength.

—ISAIAH 30:15 (NIV)

The Lord is good, a Strength and Stronghold
in the day of trouble; He knows (recognizes,
has knowledge of, and understands) those
who take refuge and trust in Him.

—NAHUM 1:7

I have [fixed my] hope on the living God,
Who is the Savior (Preserver, Maintainer,
Deliverer) of all men, especially of those who
believe (trust in, rely on, and adhere to Him).

—1 TIMOTHY 4:10

My trust and assured reliance and confident
hope is fixed in Him.

—HEBREWS 2:13

✛ Victory ✛

I have victory wherever I go.

—2 SAMUEL 8:6

Yours, O Lord, is the greatness and the power
and the glory and the victory and the majesty,
for all that is in the heavens and the earth is
Yours; Yours is the kingdom, O Lord, and
Yours it is to be exalted as Head over all.

—1 CHRONICLES 29:11

The Lord takes pleasure in His people; He
beautifies the humble with salvation and
adorns the wretched with victory.

—PSALM 149:4

By wise counsel I can wage war, and in an
abundance of counselors there is victory and
safety.

—PROVERBS 24:6

Amid all these things, I am more than a conqueror and gain a surpassing victory through Him Who loves me.

—ROMANS 8:37

When this perishable puts on the imperishable and this that was capable of dying puts on freedom from death, then shall be fulfilled the Scripture that says, Death is swallowed up (utterly vanquished forever) in and unto victory. . . . I thank God, Who gives me the victory [making me a conqueror] through the Lord Jesus Christ.

—1 CORINTHIANS 15:54, 57

Thanks be to God, Who in Christ always leads me in triumph [as a trophy of Christ's victory] and through me spreads and makes evident the fragrance of the knowledge of God everywhere.

—2 CORINTHIANS 2:14

Everyone who believes that Jesus is the Christ is a child of God. And everyone who loves the Father loves his children, too. I know I love God's children if I love God and obey his commandments. Loving God means keeping his commandments, and that isn't difficult. For every child of God defeats this evil world by trusting Christ to give the victory. And the ones who win this battle against the world are the ones who believe that Jesus is the Son of God.

—1 JOHN 5:1-5 (NLT)

❧ Waiting on God and His Timing ❧

Guide me in Your truth and faithfulness and teach me, for You are the God of my salvation; for You [You only and altogether] do I wait [expectantly] all the day long.

—PSALM 25:5

I trusted in, relied on, and was confident in You, O Lord; I said, You are my God. My times are in Your hands.

—PSALM 31:14-15

I am still and rest in the Lord; I wait for Him and patiently lean myself upon Him; I fret not myself because of him who prospers in his way, because of the man who brings wicked devices to pass.

—PSALM 37:7

And now, Lord, what do I wait for and expect? My hope and expectation are in You.

Deliver me from all my transgressions; make me not the scorn and reproach of the [self-confident] fool!

—PSALM 39:7-8

I stand silently before the Lord, waiting for him to rescue me. For salvation comes from him alone. Yes, he alone is my Rock, my rescuer, defense and fortress. Why then should I be tense with fear when troubles come?

—PSALM 62:1-2 (TLB)

My eyes wait for You [looking, watching, and expecting] and You give me food in due season. You open Your hand and satisfy me with favor.

—PSALM 145:15-16

The Lord [earnestly] waits [expecting, looking, and longing] to be gracious to me; and therefore He lifts Himself up, that He may have mercy on me and show loving-kindness to me. For the Lord is a God of justice. Blessed (happy, fortunate, to be envied) are all those who [earnestly] wait for Him, who expect and look and long for Him [for His victory, His favor, His love, His peace, His joy, and His matchless, unbroken companionship]!

—ISAIAH 30:18

As I wait for the Lord [expecting, looking for, and hoping in Him] I shall change and renew my strength and power; I shall lift my wings and mount up [close to God] as eagles [mount up to the sun]; I shall run and not be weary, I shall walk and not faint or become tired.

—ISAIAH 40:31

But these things I plan won't happen right away. Slowly, steadily, surely, the time approaches when the vision will be fulfilled.

If it seems slow, do not despair, for these
things will surely come to pass. Just be
patient! They will not be overdue a single
day!

—HABAKKUK 2:3 (TLB)

❖ Walking in Love ❖

What does the Lord my God require of me but [reverently] to fear the Lord my God, [that is] to walk in all His ways, and to love Him, and to serve the Lord my God with all my [mind and] heart and with my entire being.

—DEUTERONOMY 10:12

God has given me one new commandment that I should love others just as He has loved me.

—JOHN 13:34

I walk in love because God appeals to and begs me to walk (lead a life) worthy of the [divine] calling to which I have been called [with behavior that is a credit to the summons to God's service, living as becomes me] with complete lowliness of mind (humility) and meekness (unselfishness, gentleness, mildness), with patience, bearing with others and making allowances because I love them.

—EPHESIANS 4:1-2

I walk in love, [esteeming and delighting in others] as Christ loved me and gave Himself up for me, a slain offering and sacrifice to God [for me, so that it became] a sweet fragrance.

—EPHESIANS 5:2

Above all that I put on, I put on love. I clothe myself with behavior marked by mercy, tender hearted pity, kind feeling, a lowly opinion of myself, gentle ways [and] patience. I have the power to endure whatever comes with good temper. I am gentle and forbearing with others and, if I have a difference or a grievance with someone; even as the Lord has [freely] forgiven me, I also forgive others.

—COLOSSIANS 3:12-14

Let us love one another, for love is from God; and he who loves [his fellowman] is born of God and is progressively coming to know and understand God. He who does not love has not become acquainted with God [does not and never did know Him].

—1 JOHN 4:7-8

When I walk in love God is present.

—1 JOHN 4:12

Love has been perfected in me in this: that I may have boldness in the day of judgment; because as He is, so am I in this world. There is no fear in love; but perfect love casts out fear, because fear involves torment. But he who fears has not been made perfect in love. I love Him because He first loved me.

—1 JOHN 4:17-19 (NKJV)

⁂ Wisdom ⁂

The reverent fear and worship of the Lord is
the beginning of Wisdom and skill [the pre-
ceding and the first essential, the prerequisite
and the alphabet]; a good understanding,
wisdom, and meaning have all those who do
[the will of the Lord].

—PSALM 111:10

The wise also will hear and increase in learning, and the person of understanding will
acquire skill and attain to sound counsel [so
that he may be able to steer his course
rightly].

—PROVERBS 1:5

If I receive God's words and treasure up His
commandments within me, making my ear
attentive to skillful and godly Wisdom and
inclining and directing my heart and mind to
understanding [applying all my powers to the

quest for it]; yes, if I cry out for insight and raise my voice for understanding, if I seek [Wisdom] as for silver and search for skillful and godly Wisdom as for hidden treasures, then I will understand the reverent and worshipful fear of the Lord and find the knowledge of [our omniscient] God.

—PROVERBS 2:1-5

I lean on, trust in, and am confident in the Lord with all my heart and mind and do not rely on my own insight or understanding. In all my ways I know, recognize, and acknowledge Him, and He directs and makes straight and plain my paths. I am not wise in my own eyes, but I reverently fear and worship the Lord.

—PROVERBS 3:5-7

Happy is the man who finds wisdom, and the man who gains understanding; for her proceeds are better than the profits of silver, and her gain than fine gold. She is more precious than rubies, and all the things you may desire cannot compare with her.

—PROVERBS 3:13-15 (NKJV)

I and all who are wise shall inherit glory (all honor and good) but shame is the highest rank conferred on [self-confident] fools.

—PROVERBS 3:35

I seek skillful and godly wisdom, it is better than rubies or pearls, and all the things that may be desired are not to be compared with it.

—PROVERBS 8:11

Whoever finds wisdom finds life and receives favor from the Lord. I find wisdom, and I find life and receive favor from the Lord.

—PROVERBS 8:35 (NIV)

I hear counsel, receive instruction, and accept correction, that I may be wise in the time to come.

—PROVERBS 19:20

When I am deficient in wisdom, I ask of the giving God [Who gives] to everyone liberally and ungrudgingly, without reproaching or faultfinding, and it will be given to me.

—JAMES 1:5

❧ Worship ❧

As for me, I will enter the Lord's house
through the abundance of His steadfast love
and mercy; I will worship toward and at His
holy temple in reverent fear and awe of Him.

—PSALM 5:7

All the ends of the earth shall remember and
turn to the Lord, and all the families of the
nations shall bow down and worship before
Him.

—PSALM 22:27

I know the secret [of the sweet, satisfying
companionship] of the Lord because I fear
(revere and worship) Him, and He shows me
His covenant and reveals to me its [deep,
inner] meaning.

—PSALM 25:14

I give the Lord the glory due to His name; I worship the Lord in the beauty of holiness or in holy array.

—PSALM 29:2

The Lord establishes His word and confirms His promise to me. He is for those who reverently fear and devotedly worship Him.

—PSALM 119:38

I am not wise in my own eyes. I reverently fear and worship the Lord and turn [entirely] away from evil.

—PROVERBS 3:7

I know that whatever God does, it endures forever; nothing can be added to it nor anything taken from it. And God does it so that I will [reverently] fear Him [revere and worship Him, knowing that He is].

—ECCLESIASTES 3:14

God is a Spirit (a spiritual Being) and I
worship Him in spirit and in truth (reality).

—JOHN 4:24

I make a decisive dedication of my body
[presenting all my members and faculties] as
a living sacrifice, holy (devoted, consecrated)
and well pleasing to God, which is my
reasonable (rational, intelligent) service and
spiritual worship.

—ROMANS 12:1

I am the true circumcision, who worships
God in spirit and by the Spirit of God and
exult and glory and pride myself in Jesus
Christ, and put no confidence or dependence
[on what I am] in the flesh and on outward
privileges and physical advantages and
external appearances.

—PHILIPPIANS 3:3

I receive a kingdom that is firm and stable
and cannot be shaken, and offer to God
pleasing service and acceptable worship,
with modesty and pious care and godly fear
and awe.

—HEBREWS 12:28

About the Author

JOYCE MEYER is one of the world's leading practical Bible teachers. A #1 *New York Times* bestselling author, she has written more than 100 inspirational books, including *The Confident Woman, I Dare You,* the entire Battlefield of the Mind family of books, her first venture into fiction with *The Penny,* and many others. She has also released thousands of audio teachings as well as a complete video library. Joyce's *Enjoying Everyday Life®* radio and television programs are broadcast around the world, and she travels extensively conducting conferences. Joyce and her husband, Dave, are the parents of four grown children and make their home in St. Louis, Missouri.

TO CONTACT THE AUTHOR,
PLEASE WRITE:

Joyce Meyer Ministries
P.O. Box 655
Fenton, MO 63026
USA
(636) 349-0303
www.joycemeyer.org

Joyce Meyer Ministries—Canada
P.O. Box 7700
Vancouver, BC V6B 4E2
Canada
(800) 868-1002

Joyce Meyer Ministries—Australia
Locked Bag 77
Mansfield Delivery Centre
Queensland 4122
Australia
(07) 3349 1200

Joyce Meyer Ministries—England
P.O. Box 1549
Windsor SL4 1GT
United Kingdom
01753 831102

Joyce Meyer Ministries—South Africa
P.O. Box 5
Cape Town 8000
South Africa
(27) 21-701-1056

OTHER BOOKS BY
JOYCE MEYER

JOYCE MEYER SPANISH TITLES

Come la Galleta ... Compra los Zapatos
(Eat the Cookie ... Buy the Shoes)

El Campo de Batalla de la Mente
(Battlefield of the Mind)

La Revolución de Amor (The Love Revolution)

Las Siete Cosas Que Te Roban el Gazo
(Seven Things That Steal Your Joy)

Pensamientos de Poder (Power Thoughts)

BOOKS BY DAVE MEYER

Life Lines

* Study guide available for this title